PUBLIC-PRIVATE SOLUTIONS TO EDUCATING A CYBER WORKFORCE

JOINT HEARING

BEFORE THE

SUBCOMMITTEE ON CYBERSECURITY AND INFRASTRUCTURE PROTECTION

OF THE

COMMITTEE ON HOMELAND SECURITY HOUSE OF REPRESENTATIVES

AND THE

SUBCOMMITTEE ON HIGHER EDUCATION AND WORKFORCE DEVELOPMENT

OF THE

COMMITTEE ON EDUCATION AND THE WORKFORCE HOUSE OF REPRESENTATIVES

ONE HUNDRED FIFTEENTH CONGRESS

FIRST SESSION

OCTOBER 24, 2017

Serial Nos. 115–34 and 115–38

Printed for the use of the Committee on Homeland Security

Available via the World Wide Web: http://www.govinfo.gov and
http://edworkforce.house.gov

U.S. GOVERNMENT PUBLISHING OFFICE

28–821 PDF   WASHINGTON : 2018

COMMITTEE ON HOMELAND SECURITY

MICHAEL T. MCCAUL, Texas, *Chairman*

LAMAR SMITH, Texas
PETER T. KING, New York
MIKE ROGERS, Alabama
JEFF DUNCAN, South Carolina
LOU BARLETTA, Pennsylvania
SCOTT PERRY, Pennsylvania
JOHN KATKO, New York
WILL HURD, Texas
MARTHA MCSALLY, Arizona
JOHN RATCLIFFE, Texas
DANIEL M. DONOVAN, JR., New York
MIKE GALLAGHER, Wisconsin
CLAY HIGGINS, Louisiana
JOHN H. RUTHERFORD, Florida
THOMAS A. GARRETT, JR., Virginia
BRIAN K. FITZPATRICK, Pennsylvania
RON ESTES, Kansas

BENNIE G. THOMPSON, Mississippi
SHEILA JACKSON LEE, Texas
JAMES R. LANGEVIN, Rhode Island
CEDRIC L. RICHMOND, Louisiana
WILLIAM R. KEATING, Massachusetts
DONALD M. PAYNE, JR., New Jersey
FILEMON VELA, Texas
BONNIE WATSON COLEMAN, New Jersey
KATHLEEN M. RICE, New York
J. LUIS CORREA, California
VAL BUTLER DEMINGS, Florida
NANETTE DIAZ BARRAGÁN, California

BRENDAN P. SHIELDS, *Staff Director*
STEVEN S. GIAIER, *Deputy Chief Counsel*
MICHAEL S. TWINCHEK, *Chief Clerk*
HOPE GOINS, *Minority Staff Director*

SUBCOMMITTEE ON CYBERSECURITY AND INFRASTRUCTURE PROTECTION

JOHN RATCLIFFE, Texas, *Chairman*

JOHN KATKO, New York
DANIEL M. DONOVAN, JR., New York
MIKE GALLAGHER, Wisconsin
THOMAS A. GARRETT, JR., Virginia
BRIAN K. FITZPATRICK, Pennsylvania
MICHAEL T. MCCAUL, Texas *(ex officio)*

CEDRIC L. RICHMOND, Louisiana
SHEILA JACKSON LEE, Texas
JAMES R. LANGEVIN, Rhode Island
VAL BUTLER DEMINGS, Florida
BENNIE G. THOMPSON, Mississippi *(ex officio)*

KRISTEN M. DUNCAN, *Subcommittee Staff Director*

COMMITTEE ON EDUCATION AND THE WORKFORCE

VIRGINIA FOXX, North Carolina, *Chairwoman*

JOE WILSON, South Carolina
DUNCAN HUNTER, California
DAVID P. ROE, Tennessee
GLENN "GT" THOMPSON, Pennsylvania
TIM WALBERG, Michigan
BRETT GUTHRIE, Kentucky
TODD ROKITA, Indiana
LOU BARLETTA, Pennsylvania
LUKE MESSER, Indiana
BRADLEY BYRNE, Alabama
DAVID BRAT, Virginia
GLENN GROTHMAN, Wisconsin
ELISE STEFANIK, New York
RICK W. ALLEN, Georgia
JASON LEWIS, Minnesota
FRANCIS ROONEY, Florida
PAUL MITCHELL, Michigan
TOM GARRETT, JR., Virginia
LLOYD K. SMUCKER, Pennsylvania
A. DREW FERGUSON, IV, Georgia
RON ESTES, Kansas
KAREN HANDEL, Georgia

ROBERT C. "BOBBY" SCOTT, Virginia, *Ranking Member*
SUSAN A. DAVIS, California
RAÚL M. GRIJALVA, Arizona
JOE COURTNEY, Connecticut
MARCIA L. FUDGE, Ohio
JARED POLIS, Colorado
GREGORIO KILILI CAMACHO SABLAN, Northern Mariana Islands
FREDERICA S. WILSON, Florida
SUZANNE BONAMICI, Oregon
MARK TAKANO, California
ALMA S. ADAMS, North Carolina
MARK DESAULNIER, California
DONALD NORCROSS, New Jersey
LISA BLUNT ROCHESTER, Delaware
RAJA KRISHNAMOORTHI, Illinois
CAROL SHEA-PORTER, New Hampshire
ADRIANO ESPAILLAT, New York

BRANDON RENZ, *Staff Director*
DENISE FORTE, *Minority Staff Director*

SUBCOMMITTEE ON HIGHER EDUCATION AND WORKFORCE DEVELOPMENT

BRETT GUTHRIE, Kentucky, *Chairman*

GLENN "GT" THOMPSON, Pennsylvania
LOU BARLETTA, Pennsylvania
LUKE MESSER, Indiana
BRADLEY BYRNE, Alabama
GLENN GROTHMAN, Wisconsin
ELISE STEFANIK, New York
RICK W. ALLEN, Georgia
JASON LEWIS, Minnesota
PAUL MITCHELL, Michigan
TOM GARRETT, JR., Virginia
LLOYD K. SMUCKER, Pennsylvania
RON ESTES, Kansas

SUSAN A. DAVIS, California, *Ranking Member*
JOE COURTNEY, Connecticut
ALMA S. ADAMS, North Carolina
MARK DESAULNIER, California
RAJA KRISHNAMOORTHI, Illinois
JARED POLIS, Colorado
GREGORIO KILILI CAMACHO SABLAN, Northern Mariana Islands
MARK TAKANO, California
LISA BLUNT ROCHESTER, Delaware
ADRIANO ESPAILLAT, New York

CONTENTS

PUBLIC-PRIVATE SOLUTIONS TO EDUCATING A CYBER WORKFORCE

Tuesday, October 24, 2017

U.S. HOUSE OF REPRESENTATIVES,
COMMITTEE ON HOMELAND SECURITY,
SUBCOMMITTEE ON CYBERSECURITY AND
INFRASTRUCTURE PROTECTION, JOINT WITH THE
COMMITTEE ON EDUCATION AND WORKFORCE,
SUBCOMMITTEE ON HIGHER EDUCATION
AND WORKFORCE DEVELOPMENT,
WASHINGTON, DC.

The Subcommittee on Cybersecurity and Infrastructure Protection and Subcommittee on Higher Education and Workforce Development met, pursuant to notice, at 2:06 p.m., in room 210, Rayburn House Visitors Center, Hon. John Ratcliffe [Chairman of the Cybersecurity and Infrastructure subcommittee] presiding.

Present from the Cybersecurity and Infrastructure Protection subcommittee: Representatives Ratcliffe, Donovan, and Langevin.

Present from the Education and Workforce Development subcommittee: Representatives Guthrie, Davis, Thompson, Smucker, Estes, Courtney, Adams, Takano, Rochester, and Scott.

Mr. RATCLIFFE [presiding]. Good afternoon. The Committee on Homeland Security Subcommittee on Cybersecurity and Infrastructure Protection and the Committee on Education Workforce Subcommittee on Higher Education and Workforce Development will come to order.

The subcommittees are jointly meeting today to receive testimony regarding the public-private solutions to educating a cyber work force. I now recognize myself for an opening statement.

Let me begin by welcoming our witness panel and our guests today. Thank you all for taking time away from your important work to testify here and help Congress better understand these work force issues. I am especially grateful for the opportunity to collaborate today with the Members of the Higher Education and Workforce Development Subcommittee to hold this joint hearing on developing our Nation's cyber work force.

I would like to thank Chairwoman Fox and Chairman Guthrie, as well as Ranking Members Scott and Davis for their collective work on this critical issue. It is an important time for cooperation here on Capitol Hill. It is my sincere hope that the public will be encouraged that Members on both sides of the aisle are focused on the important issues that really matter.

Cybersecurity is an issue that affects every sector of our economy and every sector of our society. The risks are broadly shared, and this joint hearing shows the need for an integrated approach to address the challenge of the cyber skills gap.

Cyber attacks are growing in frequency and sophistication, but the availability of qualified cybersecurity professionals to deal with these challenges is simply not keeping pace. We cannot speak to the shortage of workers without recognizing the importance of the academic pipeline that produces today's work force, as well as our next generation of experts who will need to keep pace with the technology and the ever-evolving threats.

The dearth of cybersecurity talent is a major resource constraint that impacts our ability to protect information and assets. More than 200,000 cybersecurity jobs in the United States are unfilled, and the demand for positions, like the information security professionals, is expected to grow by as much as 53 percent through 2018. This slow-moving crisis is very likely only to get worse.

The Cybersecurity and Infrastructure Protection Subcommittee recently heard testimony that indicated that the struggle to find qualified personnel to fill these cybersecurity roles in Government and business is not only a short-term problem, but is expected to grow and become more acute in the future. Technology innovation and criminal tactics move very fast. With each new wirelessly-connected baby monitor or internet-connected energy-efficient pipeline that comes on-line, new threats and vulnerabilities emerge to exploit those technologies.

Just as the connected world expands and new products improve our quality of life, simplifying many tasks, our vulnerabilities move in parallel and demand a skilled work force who can protect the functionality and preserve confidentiality data. Public and private hiring systems must likewise shift and adapt to a new way of thinking about hiring and recruiting. We need intellectual capital that better reflects the qualifications and skills of a new type of cyber worker.

For their entire lives, younger Americans entering the work force have possessed more technology in a single smartphone than some ever imagined. Consider that the iPhone 7 operates at 1.4 gigahertz and can process instructions at a rate of approximately 1.2 instructions every cycle in each of its two cores. Put simply, the iPhone 7s clock is 32,600 times faster than the best Apollo-era computers and could perform instructions 120 million times faster. You wouldn't be wrong in saying that an iPhone could be used to guide 120 million Apollo-era spacecraft to the moon all at the same time. The rate of innovation in the information technology sector is truly astonishing.

I believe that the Federal Government and our cybersecurity leaders can create more alliances with community groups, universities, and career and technical schools to better develop our talent pipeline. The Department of Homeland Security supports a number of efforts to strengthen its work force from programs to recruit new cyber talent to those that allow the private-sector experts the opportunity to share their knowledge with those working at DHS.

We need to encourage Government, university, employer collaborations that are meaningful and that are robust. Demonstrating cyber know-how no longer comes in discrete forms such as having a bachelor's degree or not or obtaining a cyber certification. Cyber competitions, bug bounty programs, and coding camps are all new forms of work force development.

I am looking forward to discussing with our witnesses today some of the best practices in building public-private partnerships to expand the cyber work force pipeline. The cyber capabilities of our work force help support economic strength and sustain our technological advantage. It is my firm belief that America will only remain the world's preeminent superpower so long as it remains the world's cybersecurity leader. Leadership matters, and if we don't encourage and develop the talented women and men who lead this work, we will be both poorer and less safe as a country.

[The statement of Chairman Ratcliffe follows:]

STATEMENT OF CHAIRMAN JOHN RATCLIFFE

OCTOBER 24, 2017

Let me begin by welcoming our witness panel and our guests today. Thank you for taking the time away from your important work to testify and help Congress better understand these work force issues. I am especially grateful for the opportunity to collaborate with the Members of the Higher Education and Workforce Development Subcommittee to hold this joint hearing on developing our Nation's cyber work force. I would like to thank Chairwoman Foxx and Chairman Guthrie for their work on this critical issue. It is an important time for cooperation here on Capitol Hill and it is my sincere hope that the public will be encouraged that Members on both sides of the aisle are focused on important issues that really matter.

Cybersecurity is an issue that affects every sector of our economy and our society. The risks are broadly shared and this joint hearing shows the need for an integrated approach to address the challenge of the cyber skills gap. Cyber attacks are growing in frequency and sophistication, but the availability of qualified cybersecurity professionals to deal with these challenges is not keeping pace. We cannot speak to the shortage of workers without recognizing the importance of the academic pipeline that produces today's work force as well our next generation of experts who will need to keep pace with technology and the ever-evolving threats.

The dearth of cybersecurity talent is a major resource constraint that impacts our ability to protect information and assets. More than 200,000 cybersecurity jobs in the United States are unfilled and the demand for positions, like information security professionals, is expected to grow by 53 percent through 2018. This slow-moving crisis is very likely to only get worse.

The Cybersecurity and Infrastructure Protection subcommittee recently heard testimony that indicated that the struggle to find qualified personnel to fill cybersecurity roles in Government and business is not only a short-term problem, but is expected to grow and become even more acute in the future. Technology innovation and criminal tactics move very fast, and with each new wirelessly-connected baby monitor or interconnected energy-efficient pipeline that comes on-line, new threats and vulnerabilities emerge to exploit those technologies. Just as the connected world expands and new products improve our quality of life, simplifying many tasks, our vulnerabilities move in parallel and demand a skilled work force who can protect the functionality and preserve confidential data.

Public and private hiring systems must likewise shift and adapt to a new way of thinking about hiring and recruiting; we need intellectual capital that better reflects the qualifications and skills of a new type of cyber worker. For their entire lives, younger Americans just entering the work force have possessed more technology in a single smartphone than some ever imagined. Consider that the iPhone 7 operates at 1.4 gigahertz and can process instructions at a rate of approximately 1.2 instructions every cycle in each of its 2 cores. Put simply, the iPhone 7's clock is 32,600 times faster than the best Apollo-era computers and could perform instructions 120,000,000 times faster. You wouldn't be wrong in saying an iPhone could be used to guide 120,000,000 Apollo-era spacecraft to the moon, all at the same time. The rate of innovation in the information technology sector is simply astonishing.

I believe the Federal Government and our cybersecurity leaders can create more alliances with community groups, universities, and career and technical schools to better develop our talent pipeline. The Department of Homeland Security supports a number of efforts to strengthen its work force, from programs to recruit new cyber talent to those that allow private-sector experts the opportunity to share their knowledge working at DHS. We need to encourage Government-university-employer collaborations that are meaningful and robust. Demonstrating cyber know how no longer comes in discrete forms such as having a bachelor's degree or not, or obtaining a cyber certification. Cyber competitions, bug bounty programs, and coding camps are all new forms of work force development.

I am looking forward to discussing with our witnesses today some of the best practices in building public-private partnerships to expand the cyber work force pipeline.

The cyber capabilities of our work force help support economic strength and sustain our technological advantage. It is my firm belief that America will only remain the world's preeminent superpower so long as it remains the world's cybersecurity leader. Leadership matters, and if we don't encourage and develop the talented men and women who lead this work, we will be both poorer and less safe.

Mr. RATCLIFFE. The Chair now recognizes the Ranking Minority Member of the Subcommittee on Cybersecurity and Infrastructure Protection, the gentleman from Louisiana, Mr. Richmond, for his opening statement.

Mr. RICHMOND. Good afternoon, and I would like to thank Chairman Ratcliffe for holding today's joint hearing to explore solutions to educating our cyber work force. I would also like to thank Subcommittee on Higher Education and Workforce Chairman Guthrie and Ranking Member Davis for participating in today's hearing and sharing your expertise with us.

Last month, we held a hearing to discuss the challenge public and private-sector groups encounter as they try to recruit and retain skilled cybersecurity professionals, including Federal agencies like DHS. Every expert on the panel seemed to agree that the real problem is demand. The need for cybersecurity talent is accelerating at an impossible rate. We cannot rely on 4-year academic institutions and traditional educational frameworks to produce a stream of professionals commensurate with the number of connected devices we now use.

What we learned is that before we can recruit and retain, we have to start with a more fundamental question—how can we educate, train, and certify today's students and job applicants to be tomorrow's cybersecurity experts? How do we inject more professionals into the job market?

In 2012, Bureau of Labor Statistics projected that by 2020 there would be 400,000 computer scientists available to fill 1.4 million computer science jobs. Recent reports suggest that that deficit is growing instead of shrinking and may reach 1.8 million by 2022. To overcome this shortage, we need a "no stone left unturned" mentality that allows us to tap into every segment of the applicant pool.

Unfortunately, that is not the case today. At our hearing last month, we heard from the International Consortium of Minority Cybersecurity Professionals, or ICMCP, that women and minorities are still vastly underrepresented in cybersecurity, with women making up around 11 percent and African-Americans and Hispanics making up less than 12 percent of the global cyber work force combined.

What those numbers say to me is that we are still leaving talent on the table. ICMCP's testimony went even further, arguing that in the realm of National statute, having a diverse cyber work force is mission-critical. To support this, ICMCP pointed to the 2014 CIA diversity and leadership study, which found that a lack of diversity in CIA's leadership may have contributed to past intelligence failures.

We need to be leveraging non-traditional training models, like apprenticeships or vocational programs, community colleges, and career development tools. We also need to grow partnerships at the K–12 level to make sure children are being introduced to computers at an early age, even the ones who go to schools that can't afford a specialized tech program.

Some of the skills we need to leverage can't be taught in a classroom, and we need to think creatively about how we identify and cultivate traits that lead themselves to cybersecurity, for example, a natural affinity for problem solving or an analytical approach to risk. With the risk access and support, these candidates can easily learn the technical skills through on-the-job training, industry certifications, community college courses, and modern vocational programs.

As our world grows more and more connected, we also need a multidisciplinary approach to cyber education, one that reaches professionals in the fields like construction, nursing, and electrical engineering. I look forward to hearing ideas from our esteemed panel of witnesses today about how we as Federal policy makers should be thinking about growing and diversifying our cyber talent pipeline. But ultimately, if we are going to make a dent in the cyber work force challenge, we need to do more than talk about it. We cannot pretend to be serious about right-sizing the cyber work force while at the same time entertaining the administration's request for massive cuts to programs like the National Science Foundation's Scholarship for Service.

Similarly, I cannot fathom what kind of message is being sent to DACA recipients working to earn tech degrees in fields like cybersecurity, nor can I understand the logic behind needlessly sending this home-grown talent abroad.

I will conclude by saying that defending our networks from cyber attacks requires strong leadership, sustained funding from Congress, and action. I look forward to hearing the testimony of our witnesses today and hope we can identify innovative ways to work together to address cybersecurity work force challenges. With that, I yield back.

[The statement of Ranking Member Richmond follows:]

STATEMENT OF RANKING MEMBER CEDRIC L. RICHMOND

OCTOBER 24, 2017

Last month, we held a hearing to discuss the challenge public and private-sector groups encounter as they try to recruit and retain skilled cybersecurity professionals—including Federal agencies like DHS.

Every expert on the panel seemed to agree that the real problem is demand: The need for cybersecurity talent is accelerating at an impossible rate. We cannot rely on 4-year academic institutions and traditional educational frameworks to produce a stream of professionals commensurate with the number of connected devices we now use.

What we learned is that, before we can recruit and retain, we have to start with a more fundamental question—how can we educate, train, and certify today's students and job applicants to be tomorrow's cybersecurity experts? How do we inject more professionals into the job market?

In 2012, the Bureau of Labor Statistics projected that by 2020, there would be 400,000 computer scientists available to fill 1.4 million computer science jobs. Recent reports suggest that deficit is growing instead of shrinking, and may reach 1.8 million by 2022. To overcome this shortage, we need a "no stone left unturned" mentality that allows us to tap into every segment of the applicant pool.

Unfortunately, that is not the case today. At our hearing last month, we heard from the International Consortium of Minority Cybersecurity Professionals, or ICMCP, that women and minorities are still vastly under-represented in cybersecurity—with women making up around 11 percent, and African Americans and Hispanics making up less than 12 percent of the global cyber work force combined. What those numbers say to me is that we are still leaving talent on the table.

ICMCP's testimony went even further, arguing that in the realm of National security, having a diverse cyber work force is mission-critical. To support this, ICMCP pointed to the 2014 CIA Diversity in Leadership Study which found that a lack of diversity in CIA's leadership may have contributed to past intelligence failures. We need to be leveraging non-traditional training models like apprenticeships or vocational programs, community colleges, and career development tools.

We also need to grow partnerships at the K–12 level to make sure children are being introduced to computers at an earlier age—even the ones who go to schools that can't afford a specialized tech program.

Some of the skills we need to leverage can't be taught in a classroom, and we need to think creatively about how we identify and cultivate traits that lend themselves to cybersecurity—for example, a natural affinity for problem solving or an analytical approach to risk.

With the right access and support, these candidates can easily learn the technical skills through on-the-job training, industry certifications, community college courses, and modern vocational programs. As our world grows more and more connected, we also need a multidisciplinary approach to cyber education—one that reaches professionals in fields like construction, nursing, and electrical engineering.

I look forward to hearing ideas from our esteemed panel of witnesses today about how we, as Federal policy makers, should be thinking about growing and diversifying our cyber talent pipeline. But ultimately, if we're going to make a dent in the cyber work force challenge, we need to do more than talk about it.

We cannot pretend to be serious about right-sizing the cyber work force while at the same time entertaining the administration's request for massive cuts to programs like the National Science Foundation's Scholarship for Service.

Similarly, I cannot fathom what kind of message is being sent to DACA recipients working to earn tech degrees in fields like cybersecurity—nor can I understand the logic behind needlessly sending this home-grown talent abroad.

I'll conclude by saying that defending our networks from cyber attack requires strong leadership, sustained funding from Congress, and action. I look forward to hearing the testimony of our witnesses today, and hope we can identify innovative ways to work together to address cybersecurity work force challenges.

Mr. RATCLIFFE. I thank the gentleman. The Chair now recognizes the Chairman of the Subcommittee on Higher Education and Workforce Development, the gentleman from Kentucky, Mr. Guthrie, for any statement that he has.

Mr. GUTHRIE. Thank you very much. Good afternoon and welcome to today's joint subcommittee hearing with colleagues from the Subcommittee on Cybersecurity and Infrastructure Protection. I would like to thank our panel of witnesses and Chairman Ratcliffe, Ranking Member Richmond, Ranking Member Davis, and the Members of both subcommittees for joining today's important discussion on apprenticeships and opportunities for us to grow the Nation's work force.

When Americans think of data breaches and cyber attacks, names like Equifax come to mind. This and other recent high-profile data breaches have made private and sensitive information vulnerable to identity theft, as well as other cyber crimes. Cyber crimes are constantly appearing in the news, and Americans want to know what is being done to protect their data, as well as other vulnerable targets that compromise our National infrastructure.

Organizations in public and private sectors are actively seeking skilled professionals to fill the numerous jobs available in the growing cybersecurity field and are coming up short in the number of Americans able to fill these essential positions that ensure our American cyber infrastructure is safe. A recent study by the Intel Security and Center for Strategic and International Studies, CSIS, examined the global security, cybersecurity work force shortage and confirmed that the talent shortage was real and wide-spread. Eighty-two percent of participation report of a shortage of cybersecurity skills.

The same report found that more than 209,000 cybersecurity jobs in the United States are unfilled, and job postings are up 74 percent over the past 5 years. Additionally, the demand for cybersecurity professionals is expected to grow to over 1.8 million by 2022. This skills gap is not unique to cybersecurity sector. Many other industries such as manufacturing and transportation are facing a shortage of skilled workers to fill good-paying jobs. However, when dealing with the cybersecurity, the stakes are even higher, because we are dealing with National security.

Fortunately, today's hearing continues the discussion in Congress on how to best fill the skills gap. The House unanimously passed Strengthening Career and Technical Education for the 21st Century Act, which allows States to dedicate additional resources toward high-demand fields such as cybersecurity based on changing economic educational and National security needs.

Additionally, the Committee on Education and Workforce has been carefully observing the implementation of Workforce Innovation and Opportunity Act that was signed into law in 2014. This law streamlined the confusing maze of work force development programs and increased the amount of funding available to States that meet specific work force demands based on conversations with public and private stakeholders in each State. Today's hearing will examine solutions to filling the skills gap that currently exists in the cybersecurity field and how coalitions across Government, academic institutions, and private industries can pave the way to successfully close the skills gap and keep our country's cybersecurity infrastructure safe.

I look forward to hearing from our witnesses about how Congress can assist, and the conversation is already taking place between the institutions of higher education and public and private entities in the cybersecurity field. I yield back.

[The prepared statement of Chairman Guthrie follows:]

STATEMENT OF CHAIRMAN BRETT GUTHRIE

OCTOBER 24, 2017

When Americans think of data breaches and cyber attacks, names like Equifax come to mind. This and other recent high-profile data breaches have made private and sensitive information vulnerable to identity theft as well as other cyber crimes.

Cyber crimes are constantly appearing in the news, and Americans want to know what is being done to protect their data, as well as other vulnerable targets that comprise our National infrastructure.

Organizations in the public and private sectors are actively seeking skilled professionals to fill the numerous jobs available in the growing cybersecurity field, and are coming up short in the number of Americans able to fill these essential positions that ensure our American cyber infrastructure is safe.

A recent study by Intel Security and the Center for Strategic and International Studies (CSIS) examined the global cybersecurity work force shortage and confirmed that the talent shortage was real and wide-spread. Eighty-two percent of participants report a shortage of cybersecurity skills.

The same report found that more than 209,000 cybersecurity jobs in the United States are unfilled, and job postings are up 74 percent over the past 5 years. Additionally, the demand for cybersecurity professionals is expected to continue to grow to over 1.8 million by 2022.

This skills gap is not unique to the cybersecurity sector. Many other industries such as manufacturing and transportation are facing a shortage of skilled workers to fill good-paying jobs. However, when dealing with cybersecurity, the stakes are even higher because we are dealing with National security.

Fortunately, today's hearing continues the discussion in Congress on how to best fill the skills gap.

The House unanimously passed the Strengthening Career and Technical Education for the 21st Century Act, which allows States to dedicate additional resources toward high-demand fields such as cybersecurity based on changing economic, educational, or National security needs.

Additionally, the Committee on Education and the Workforce has been carefully observing the implementation of the Workforce Innovation and Opportunity Act that was signed into law in 2014.

This law streamlined the confusing maze of work force development programs, and increased the amount of funding available to the States to meet specific work force demands based on conversations with public and private stakeholders in each State.

Today's hearing will examine solutions to filling the skills gap that currently exists in the cybersecurity field, and how coalitions across Government, academic institutions, and private industries can pave the way to successfully close this skills gap and keep our country's cybersecurity infrastructure safe.

Mr. RATCLIFFE. I thank the gentleman. The Chair now recognizes the Ranking Minority Member of the Subcommittee on Higher Education and Workforce Development, the gentlelady from California, Ms. Davis, for her opening statement.

Ms. DAVIS. Thank you. Thank you, Mr. Chairman. I want to thank our presenters here this morning or this afternoon for this timely and important hearing. I am certainly excited to be joining with the Cybersecurity and Infrastructure Subcommittee, as well.

So you know, we are holding this hearing today to explore the critical issue of the cybersecurity work force pipeline. It is an urgent problem that has serious ramifications for our National security. As my colleagues have pointed out, cybersecurity attacks are on the rise, resulting in massive data breaches and the loss of critical private data, as well.

We know that cybersecurity vulnerabilities extend to critical infrastructure and even our elections. The need for a more secure cyber infrastructure is only going to grow as technology continues to move into even more aspects of our daily lives. So by tackling this problem, we can create critical infrastructure and a very important component is to also create many more high-paying jobs.

The fundamental building block of a strong and durable cyber infrastructure is highly-skilled cybersecurity workers. But there is a consensus that we face a critical shortage of cybersecurity professionals, leaving the Nation especially vulnerable. So in today's hearing, we will hear from businesses, as well as higher education institutions on what is being done, what remains to be done in order to fill our cybersecurity work force needs.

In order to address these problems, we must ensure that we are actively recruiting women, African-Americans, Hispanics, Native Americans into the field. These groups are woefully underrepresented in the cybersecurity work force. According to a study, women account for only about 11 percent to 14 percent of North America's cybersecurity professionals, so we have to do better. We must not only deepen, but also broaden the pool of highly-trained individuals in the field.

I look forward to hearing from Dr. Ralls on the many innovative programs that the Northern Virginia Community Colleges has developed to rebuild this robust cybersecurity work force. Really, in response to a burgeoning need, the college has grown from 50 to 1,500 students in one of his associate's programs in just 4 years. That is really a remarkable change and increase. They are using some very successful proven career development methods like apprenticeships, that I think we are all going to be talking about, and career and technical education to bridge the gap.

This is the type of innovation that we should promote and support, but I do want to raise a point of concern that the administration is pointing us in the wrong direction. The administration's budget request proposed to cut funding for the CyberCorps Scholarship for Service Program by a whopping 27 percent from its fiscal year 2017 levels, so we want to be looking to expand and not contract our efforts to fill cybersecurity work force shortages.

Surely Government, educational institutions, and industry leaders must come together to address the shortage. Government should be adequately investing in the educational and work force development infrastructure to grow the talent pool and raise awareness for cybersecurity careers. I know that there are innovative ways that the work force system can use Federal investment to build a strong cybersecurity work force.

In my district, in San Diego, the San Diego Workforce Partnership is using funding from the Obama administration's Tech-Hire grants to build cybersecurity training programs. I also believe that educational institutions must be more responsive to the shortages by creating an expanding cybersecurity programs. I know that we are going to have some great examples here today.

Businesses and industry leaders must also do their part, and I look forward to hearing as well from IBM. Industry leaders should be expanding apprenticeship programs, investing in retraining and upscaling their current work force, as well as recruiting from a more diverse talent pool. It is certainly goes without saying that our industry leaders must work collaborative with educational and training institutions. Businesses must also take a critical look at their hiring practices and really look at their credentialing requirements to ensure that they are not over-specifying credentials that might create a barrier.

I want to thank all of our chairs, and I look forward to our witnesses and how we can create more attractive career pathways in cybersecurity for both the civilian and the military work force. Thank you very much.

[The statement of Ranking Member Davis follows:]

STATEMENT OF RANKING MEMBER SUSAN A. DAVIS

OCTOBER 24, 2017

Thank you Mr. Chairman.

This is a timely and important hearing. I am excited to be working with our colleagues from the Cybersecurity and Infrastructure Subcommittee.

We are holding this joint hearing today to explore the critical issue of the cybersecurity work force pipeline. It is an urgent problem that has serious ramifications for our National security. As my colleagues have pointed out today, cybersecurity attacks are on the rise resulting in massive data breaches and the loss of critical private data.

And we know that cybersecurity vulnerabilities extend to critical infrastructure and our elections. The need for a more secure cyber infrastructure is only going to grow as technology continues to move into even more aspects of our daily lives. By tackling this problem we can secure critical information and create many more high-paying jobs.

The fundamental building block of a strong and durable cyber infrastructure is highly-skilled cybersecurity workers. But there's a consensus that we face a critical shortage of cybersecurity professionals, leaving the Nation especially vulnerable. In today's hearing we will hear from businesses as well as higher education institutions on what is being done, and what remains to be done in order to fill our cybersecurity work force needs.

In order to address these problems we must ensure that we are actively recruiting women, African Americans, Hispanics, and Native Americans into the field. These groups are woefully underrepresented in the cybersecurity work force. According to a recent survey, women account for only 14 percent of North America's cybersecurity professionals. We must do better than this. We must not only deepen but also broaden the pool of highly-trained individuals in the field.

I look forward to hearing from Dr. Ralls on the many innovative programs that the Northern Virginia Community College has developed to build a robust cybersecurity work force. In response to burgeoning demand, the Northern Virginia Community College has grown from 50 to 1,500 students in one of its associates programs in just 4 years—that's a remarkable thirty-fold increase. They are using successful, proven career development methods like apprenticeships and career and technical education to bridge the gap.

This is the type of innovation we should promote and support. However I am concerned that the administration is pointing us in the wrong direction. The administration's budget request proposed to cut funding for the CyberCorps Scholarship for Service program by a whopping 27 percent from its fiscal year levels. We should be looking to expand, not contract, our efforts to fill cybersecurity work force shortages.

Government, educational institutions, and industry leaders must come together to address the shortage. Government should be adequately investing in the educational and work force development infrastructure to grow the talent pool and raise awareness for cybersecurity careers. I know that there are innovative ways that the work force system can use Federal investment to build a strong cybersecurity work force. In my district, the San Diego Workforce Partnership is using funding from the Obama administration's Tech-Hire grants to build cybersecurity training programs.

I also believe that educational institutions must be more responsive to the shortages by creating and expanding cybersecurity programs and I know we have great examples here today.

Businesses and industry leaders must also do their part and I look forward to hearing today from IBM. Industry leaders should be expanding apprenticeship programs, investing in retraining and upskilling their current work force as well as recruiting from a more diverse talent pool. And it goes without saying, I hope, that our industry leaders must work collaboratively with educational and training institutions. Businesses must also take a critical look at their hiring practices and really look at their credentialing requirements to ensure that they are not over-specifying credentials that might create a barrier.

I would like to thank Chairs Ratcliffe, McCaul, and Guthrie for holding this hearing.

I look forward to hearing from the witnesses on how we can create attractive career pathways in cybersecurity for both the civilian and military work force.

Mr. RATCLIFFE. I thank the gentlelady. Other Members of the committee are reminded that their own opening statements may be submitted for the record.

[The statements of Ranking Member Thompson and Chairwoman Foxx follow:]

Statement of Ranking Member Bennie G. Thompson

October 24, 2017

According to the International Data Corporation, global revenues for cybersecurity technology and services will grow from $73.7 billion in 2016 to $101.6 billion in 2020.

Yet, a report by Frost and Sullivan and (ISC)-Squared released earlier this year predicted that, despite current projections for steady growth in cybersecurity jobs, there will be 1.5 million unfilled cybersecurity positions world-wide by 2020.

As policy makers, we have to ask ourselves why we are struggling to attract people to a field that promises so much growth.

From where I sit, I can see at least three challenges we have to address.

As a Member of Congress representing the Second Congressional District of Mississippi, I can tell you that we have to do a better job cultivating domestic cybersecurity talent.

As Ranking Member of the Committee on Homeland Security, I am worried that President Trump's immigration policies—particularly related the Deferred Action for Childhood Arrivals—will result in a loss of cybersecurity talent that our academic institutions and businesses have already spent time and money educating and training.

And as a Member of the Congressional Black Caucus, I know that we have missed opportunities to develop cybersecurity talent in diverse communities.

I am pleased that the witnesses before us today will be able to give us their thoughts on how the Federal Government can work with the private sector to address all three of these issues.

When the Cybersecurity and Infrastructure Protection Subcommittee held its hearing on cybersecurity work force challenges last month, I told the panel what my constituents in Mississippi tell me about what our approach to this problem should be: Invest aggressively in growing domestic cybersecurity talent.

As a new generation enters the work force and as displaced workers try to find their way in a changing economy, we must equip American workers with the skills they need to take advantage of cybersecurity job opportunities.

Unfortunately, the Trump administration's commitment to helping our work force gain the skills they need to compete for cybersecurity jobs is hardly consistent.

Although President Trump congratulated himself last month for directing the Department of Education to spend at least $200 million annually on STEM education grants, his fiscal year 2018 budget request slashed the National Science Foundation's Scholarship for Service Program.

And I would be remiss if I did not point out that no one knows where the Department of Education is going to get the $200 million it is supposed to spend on STEM grants.

The only thing we do know is that the President did not send any new money with his directive.

President Trump is further undermining efforts to address our cybersecurity work force challenges with his decision to allow the DACA Program to expire in March.

If we do not provide "Dreamers" a path to citizenship, we run the risk of hemorrhaging talent across a wide variety of disciplines.

I am pleased that businesses like Google, Facebook, IBM, and many others have formed the Coalition for the American Dream to advocate for a path to citizenship for "Dreamers" and to keep their talents in the United States.

I am similarly encouraged by the advocacy of academic leaders who have urged Congress to act so that the Nation can reap the benefits of the Dreamers' skills and talents.

Finally, we must do more to promote cybersecurity opportunities in diverse communities. Today, black and Hispanic people—combined—make up only 12 percent of the cybersecurity work force. To me, that means we are missing out on untapped potential.

Despite on-going challenges with a lack of consistent leadership from the White House, I am pleased that the private sector and our academic institutions continue to work together to build a robust cybersecurity work force.

I am eager to learn more about these efforts and how Congress can help support them.

———

Statement of Chairwoman Virginia Foxx

We are facing a skills gap in this country, and the cybersecurity sector is not immune from its impact.

Major corporations and Government entities are looking for highly-skilled professionals to fill important positions that ensure our country's public institutions, as well as private businesses, remain safe from the growing number of cyber threats.

According to a report by the Congressional Research Service, the Department of Defense, and the Department of Homeland Security require over 4,000 personnel to handle the current cybersecurity threats that impact the Government.

While this skills gap currently exists in the cybersecurity sector, conversations are being had between skills-based institutions of education and employers to better ensure that the skills students are learning in the classroom match the need for skilled employees in the cybersecurity filed.

This is encouraging news, and I hope the cybersecurity sector continues on this positive trend, and can be a model for other industries to prepare a skilled and equipped work force of the future.

The progress is so encouraging that a study by the RAND Corporation has indicated that demand will likely be met over time due to an increased number of cybersecurity apprenticeship and education programs.

At the Education and Workforce Committee, we are looking for more ways to raise awareness across all industries for apprenticeship and other earn-and-learn opportunities. That is why today's hearing is particularly important, not just what it means for security, but what it means for future jobs.

Mr. RATCLIFFE. We are all very pleased to have a very distinguished panel of witnesses before us today. Dr. Stephen Cambone is the associate vice chancellor for the Texas A&M University System. Good to see you again, Dr. Cambone.

Mr. Douglas Rapp is the president of Rofori Corporation-DEFCON Cyber and is testifying on behalf of the Cyber Leadership Alliance. Mr. Rapp, we are glad to have you here, as well.

Mr. David Jarvis is the security and CIO lead of the IBM Institute for Business Value. Mr. Jarvis, welcome to our committees.

Our final witness is Dr. R. Scott Ralls, president of the Northern Virginia Community College. Dr. Ralls, thank you for being here, as well.

[Witnesses sworn.]

The witnesses' full written statements will appear in the record. The Chair now recognizes Dr. Cambone for 5 minutes for his opening statement.

STATEMENT OF STEPHEN A. CAMBONE, ASSOCIATE VICE CHANCELLOR, TEXAS A&M UNIVERSITY SYSTEM

Mr. CAMBONE. Thank you, Mr. Chairman, Chairman Ratcliffe, Mr. Richmond, and Ms. Davis, it is a pleasure to be here with you. I am a relatively newly-appointed associate vice chancellor of the university, but I come to this hearing with a long background in the field, having spent a good deal of time in my prior positions dealing with the issues of both the cyber domain—that is, operations and activities in the cyber domain, including everything from your wristwatch to robots—and have spent a fair amount of time in the private sector doing the same.

A word about Texas A&M. Texas A&M is a land grant university. As such, it very closely hews to the original purpose of the land grant college, which is to look after the development of the work force. The reason I am there is the vice chancellor for engineering for the system is looking to build a coherent program in cybersecurity out of the 11 universities and 3 agencies over which she has considerable influence, because she is, as well, the dean of engineering of the college at A&M and has some 19,000 engineering students from which to cull the cybersecurity work force of the future.

We have over the past year-and-a-half been granted three designations by NSA and the Department of Homeland Security in cybersecurity. We are quite proud of that fact. It is in cyber operations, cyber defense education, and cyber defense research. What does that mean? It means essentially that the auditors came in from both DHS and NSA and said, do you have a teaching program? Do you have students? Do you have faculty who will address the issues that are going to face the country in cybersecurity in the years to come? The answer was, yes, we did, and therefore those designations are in place.

We have a minor degree program in cybersecurity for undergraduates. In the course of the last 2 years, we now have 300 students in that program, and 39 have graduated with bachelor's degrees with a minor in cybersecurity. In the spring of 2018, we will begin a master's of engineering in cybersecurity. It is a multidisciplinary degree intended to admit any bachelor's of science graduate into the program where they will learn the essentials of cybersecurity in order to bring it back to their career fields in aero, mechanical, civil. Whichever engineering field they may have been in, they will have the fundamentals in cybersecurity and be able to bring it to their businesses.

We have worked fairly hard, Mr. Richmond, to make some arrangements with our friends at Blinn College, which is a very large 2-year university in the town next to College Station. In particular, in the field of nursing, where we will work with them to put together a program to test biomedical devices, to see that they meet the standards of both users and the patients.

I wanted to offer two thoughts in closing on how we might address some of the issues associated with the work force. One is a bit wonky, I will admit, and that is that the ISACs, which are functioning better or worse depending on the sector, have a wealth of data and information within them, which we think if we could get some of the research faculty from around the country to engage the material in those ISACs, we might be able to begin to pull out some of the best practices and some of the enduring issues that need to be addressed and offer then recommendations both to the ISAC leadership and the members, but also into our academic programs as to how we might begin to address those enduring problems.

The second has to do with really picking up on the notion of a land grant college. The university is a land grant, sea grant, and space grant college. We think that it is time maybe to think about a cyber grant program and model it on the space and sea grant programs, which are really designed to be consortium-based and to be outreach-focused in a way to build up the cybersecurity practices of the people in the various regions of the country that they serve.

So with that, Mr. Chairman, thank you.

[The prepared statement of Mr. Cambone follows:]

14

INTRODUCTION

Chairman Ratcliffe, Chairman Guthrie, Members of the subcommittees, thank you for the opportunity to testify before you today.

I come before you this afternoon to discuss cybersecurity work force development, as the recently-appointed associate vice chancellor for Cyber Security Initiatives for Texas A&M University System.

The system's flagship university, Texas A&M, is a land grant university. As such it is particularly attuned to meeting the work force needs of the State and Nation.

My charge is to assist in the development of a multidisciplinary program in cybersecurity across the 11 universities and 7 State agencies that comprise the system. I have been asked to engage leaders across the State and Nation, both in the public and private sector, to identify the most pressing needs and then look to the resources of the system to determine whether and in what way we can contribute to meeting those needs.

Our objective is to develop transformational cybersecurity capabilities, implemented by a well-educated and trained work force, that support the United States' mission of protecting against and combatting large-scale cyber attacks.

I come to the Texas A&M System after a career in both the public and private sector. During my time in the Pentagon as senior official from 2001–2006, I was witness to and occasionally helpful in advancing the National interest and capabilities in the cyber domain. While serving as the first under secretary of defense, I had oversight of on behalf of the Secretary of a variety of cyber issues.

My subsequent experience in the private sector included responsibility for a substantial business unit that supported several Government customers with interests in the cyber domain. That business unit also explored as early as 2008 the use of commercial communications and devices—and their attendant security—to manage small robots and hand-held drones, controlled through cellular networks and reporting to the user on wearable devices, for a wide variety of applications.

Given our increasing reliance on cyber-physical systems—the power grid and the internet of things being two examples—there is a compelling need for well-educated professionals to address the cybersecurity needs of the Nation.

Those needs are felt at the local, Tribal, State, and Federal level. Some put the need at more than 200,000 professionals, not including the primary, secondary, or university educators.

Universities across the Nation are experimenting with a variety of undergraduate and graduate degrees and professional education programs to meet the demand.

The difficulty faced in meeting the demand is both the shortage of well-educated instructors and the increasing velocity of change in the field of cybersecurity.

Within the Texas A&M University System we are addressing both issues.

BACKGROUND ON THE TEXAS A&M UNIVERSITY SYSTEM WORK FORCE ACTIVITIES

The Texas A&M College of Engineering is one of the largest in the Nation with over 19,000 students and numerous tenure track and professional faculty conducting research and collaborating outside of Engineering on a range of cyber-related topics.

The quality of their work, and the education it supports, has resulted in Texas A&M's designation by the NSA/DHS as a National Center of Excellence in three distinct areas: Cyber Operations, Cyber Defense Education, and Cyber Defense Research.

Texas A&M University is one of only eight universities in the United States, and is the only public university in the American Association of Universities, with all three designations.

Texas A&M has created a cybersecurity minor field of study. First implemented in 2016, it is already the largest minor in the College of Engineering.

Over 300 students in six different university colleges/schools have enrolled, including 39 who have already graduated.

In the spring of 2018, the University will enroll its first cohort of students in a distinctive Masters of Engineering in Cybersecurity.

In addition, the Texas A&M Engineering Extension Service (TEEX), and the Texas A&M Engineering Experiment Station (TEES), two State agencies which are a part of the Texas A&M University System, have extensive programs in applied research and emergency response work force development related to cybersecurity.

TEEX is a leading member of the National Domestic Preparedness Consortium and the National Cybersecurity Preparedness Consortium. Both consortia are critical preparedness partners of DHS/FEMA. Its Cyber Readiness Center provides technical assistance to private and public organizations with the intent of improving the health and security of their digital operations. It delivers, at no cost, DHS/ FEMA cybersecurity courses. It provides preparatory classes for professional certifications in cybersecurity and provides technical assistance to prepare for cyber events. And, it conducts response exercises to prepared communities and their officials to take swift, targeted action to address an attack and limit losses.

TEES, through its EDGE program for professional and continuing education, supports the deployment of face-to-face, on-line and blended classes. All of its courses can be made portable. In addition, it has developed the means of providing similar services for academic instruction, enabling coursework to be presented throughout the Texas A&M University System. These assets are being woven into the cybersecurity initiatives sponsored by the vice chancellor's office.

As impressive and effective as these measures and similar efforts made in States across the Nation may be, they are not sufficient to meet the increasing need for a well-educated cybersecurity work force.

RECOMMENDATIONS

With your permission, I'd like to offer two suggestions that might improve the rate at which we educate and increase the cyber work force.

Expand existing information-sharing programs to meet work force needs

DHS might select and invite researchers and educators to affiliate with each existing ISAC and ISAO, expanding the collaborative benefits of these public-private partnerships to include cyber work force development.

Participants from higher education would be exposed to and able to conduct basic and applied research into each sector's immediate challenges. This research can benefit each sector and might be shared across sectors while simultaneously providing material for real-time updates of course curriculum. This practical knowledge could help our graduates entering the work force to be "job ready on Day 1".

Create a Cyber Grant program to meet work force needs

The Morrill Act recognized that the classical education then offered by institutions of higher learning were not meeting the pressing needs of the Nation. It gave rise to the great land grant universities in the United States. More recently, Congress created Sea and Space Grant programs to conduct research and extend the benefits of that education to local populations.

Considering the challenges we face in developing and maintaining the cybersecurity work force, the creation of a Cyber Grant Program modeled after the three previous grant programs can be established to realize similar benefits.

It can facilitate significant advancement of cybersecurity research, education, and outreach across a broad front, including the development and delivery of portable course content that addresses all 16 critical infrastructure sectors designated by DHS, and can be used by industry in professional development.

CONCLUSION

It will take time to build the cyber work force we require. We need to be intentional and aggressive in our efforts now to yield essential returns in the future. Time is of the essence and the Texas A&M University System is ready to serve.

Mr. RATCLIFFE. Thank you, Dr. Cambone. The Chair now recognizes Mr. Rapp for 5 minutes for his opening statement.

STATEMENT OF DOUGLAS C. RAPP, PRESIDENT, ROFORI CORPORATION-DEFCON CYBER, TESTIFYING ON BEHALF OF THE CYBER LEADERSHIP ALLIANCE

Mr. RAPP. Thank you, Chairman Ratcliffe, Chairman Guthrie, Mr. Richmond, and Ms. Davis, for this opportunity to come here and testify in front of you on this very important topic of public-private partnerships and work force development. I am here representing the Cyber Leadership Alliance, which is a 501(c)(6) professional nonprofit organization. It represents about $20 billion worth of Indiana thought leadership and industry. So we are dedicated to solving the work force deficit through public-private partnerships.

I would like to start my testimony by telling a story that really illustrates the perspective from which we come from, and that is, my own son, Urban, went to a public school, a great public school in Indiana. While he was there, he was an average student. That is much better than I did when I was growing up, so I was OK with that.

So he was an average student and he came out of that high school. One day, I came downstairs and he was on the computer, and I asked him, what are you doing? He said, well, a couple of friends of mine, we rented some server space and we have taken a bunch of modules off of Gary's mod and we have programmed them all together, and right now we are hosting a game for people all around the world.

So I asked him, well, where in the world did you get interested in something like that? Where did you learn how to do it? His answer to me was YouTube University. So—now, that is by far the cheapest university I have paid for to date.

The point that I am trying to illustrate is that when we think about solutions to work force and how we learn, we need to be creative and disruptive when necessary. We need to look at new concepts such as proposals to use coding as a foreign language requirement in school, for new approaches, like the National Minority and Technology Council's concept of resource centers to reach out to underserved communities. We need to think about tying our data from our skill-producing institutions, our higher education directly to the employers.

We do things at Cyber Leadership Alliance, being a 501(c)(6), we positioned ourselves to be kind of a neutral ground between academia, industry, and Government, where we can take subject-matter expertise from across different verticals and bring them together to solve these problems where we are less threatened by individual motivations or agendas.

We believe that these public-private partnerships have to provide value to their partners. So it is difficult to ask a private industry to take part in something that takes them away from providing value for their shareholders. So we have to be conscious of what they must do to stay in business.

We also think that it is important to capitalize on each other's skills and expertise, and that way we can reduce redundancy, we can operate more efficiently, and we can capitalize on the subject-matter expertise of the individuals and the partnership.

So I look forward to answering any questions that you may have for me today, and thank you for having me.

[The prepared statement of Mr. Rapp follows:]

PREPARED STATEMENT OF DOUGLAS C. RAPP

OCTOBER 24, 2017

Thank you, Chairman Ratcliff and Chairman Guthrie and Members of the Homeland Security Subcommittee on Cybersecurity and Infrastructure Protection and Subcommittee on Higher Education and Workforce Development of the Committee on Education and Workforce for holding today's hearing on the extremely important topic of Public-Private Solutions to Educating a Cyber Workforce. As technology continues to connect us in ways that create synergy and solve complex problems more efficiently, so must we connect our public and private organizations to do the same. By integrating, understanding, and accepting our respective capabilities and differences, we can solve the difficult problem of educating a modern cyber work force quicker and more efficiently. The Cyber Leadership Alliance, a 501c6 industry non-profit that represents the cybersecurity thought leadership of more than $20 billion dollars of Indiana industry, is dedicated to finding solutions to reducing the cybersecurity work force deficit through effective use of public-private partnerships.

INDIANA: A CASE STUDY IN CYBER PARTNERSHIP

Indiana has long recognized the value of public-private partnerships. One need only to look at the Office of the Indiana Secretary of Commerce to see an example of a successful and enduring public-private partnership. Other successful public-private partnerships span utilities, emergency response, and other areas.

Indiana is a State of collaboration that has figured out how to bring stakeholders to the table specifically in cybersecurity. Indiana has built coalitions across Government, military, and industry to take a holistic approach to cybersecurity. Five specific examples of cybersecurity public-private partnerships are illustrated below:

Indiana National Guard Cyber Incident Response Plan.—The Indiana National Guard Cyber Incident Response Plan was the first integrated response plan in the State targeted at a State-wide cybersecurity incident. Through public-private collaboration during development, this plan was developed to define the role of State military cyber assets while coordinating the integration of State military, public, and the private sectors.

Indiana National Guard Cybersecurity Working Group.—The Indiana National Guard Cyber Security Working group was the State's first formal public-private group to meet on a consistent basis and share information regarding significant cybersecurity issues. The group initially consisted of public entities such as the National Guard, Indiana Department of Homeland Security, the Indiana Utility Regulatory Commission, FBI, and others. Private entities followed including Rook Security, Vespa Group, Pondurance, and Citizens Energy to name a few. This group no longer exists as three separate initiatives have arisen to fulfill the functions that were identified in this group.

Crit-Ex (Critical Infrastructure Exercise).—Crit-Ex was sponsored by the Indiana Department of Homeland Security, Indiana Office of Technology, the Indiana National Guard and was managed by the Cyber Leadership Alliance. The event, which is the first of its kind, brought together 2 Federal agencies, 8 State agencies, and 15 private-sector organizations. The exercise was formulated to explore the intersection between critical infrastructure and cybersecurity. Partnerships between the Government agencies and private organizations made during the exercise are helping prevent major incidents in our current high-threat environment. An important footnote is that while Crit-Ex was groundbreaking and spawned other initiatives, it has not been repeated in Indiana due to lack of funding and competing demands on Government resources.

Indiana Cybersecurity Economic Development Plan.—In 2016, the Secretary of Commerce of the State of Indiana Victor Smith, directed the creation of a State Cybersecurity Economic Development Plan as a component of his economic development strategic sector plan. Completed in early 2018, the plan was created by 19 noted subject-matter experts with input gathered during 7 cybersecurity town halls around the State of Indiana. Input from over 200 stakeholders from private industry, academia, Government, and the military provided the data that shaped the final report. The plan gives significant attention to cyber work force development and recognizes it as one of strategic 5 Lines of Effort. The report has been published and is currently available from the Indiana Department of Workforce Development (IEDC).

Indiana Executive Council on Cybersecurity.—The Indiana Executive Council on Cybersecurity can be traced back through the working group for the Crit-Ex initiative to the Indiana National Guard Cybersecurity Working Group. The counsel, created by Executive Order under former Governor Mike Pence and continued by Governor Eric Holcomb is made up of government (local, State, and Federal), private-sector, military, research, and academic stakeholders. The mandate of the counsel is to collaboratively increase Indiana's cybersecurity posture and maturity. With 28 Council members, 9 subcommittees, and more than 150 advisory members, the Council's first deliverable is a comprehensive strategy plan to Governor Holcomb by September 2018. One of the council's focus areas is cyber work force development.

Currently, Indiana is approaching the shortage of cybersecurity work force professionals like many other States—through its academic institutions. Indiana currently has 31 higher education institutions that offer cybersecurity education, 6 R1–R3 Research Centers, and 7 DHS/NSA Cybersecurity Centers of Excellence. However, the Cyber Leadership Alliance believes that the popular methodology of recruiting self-selected college-trained graduates to meet the cyber work force demands is not only flawed but rather that anyone suggesting that as a solution is at best incapable of simple math. A visit to CyberSeek.org, an on-line cybersecurity work force development tool created in a public-private partnership between the National Initiative for Cybersecurity Education (NICE), Comp-TIA, and Burning Glass will immediately invalidate that solution.

The partners within the Cyber Leadership Alliance believe that the most effective way to address the current cybersecurity talent crisis is by taking a holistic approach. Only by creating and following a long-term process of "growing your own" can you solve this problem. We have modeled that process and are currently proposing it to the Indiana Department of Workforce Development in the form of an application for a SkillUp! grant.

THE CYBER LEADERSHIP ALLIANCE SKILLUP! SOLUTION

The SkillUp! proposal is governed by a public-private partnership referred to as the Cyber Leadership Alliance Coalition (CLAC) and plans to inform, educate, grow, and retain an Indiana-based work force, with jobs awaiting them post-(re)training at the most critical levels of commerce. The SkillUp! solution is based on the following tenants:

Cybersecurity Workforce Development efforts must be driven by public-private partnerships.—No one private entity, industry sector, branch, or level of Government should attempt to "own" cybersecurity.

Cyber Public-Private partnerships should be run by or always include non-profit industry organizations.—These organizations provide a neutral ground where the direction of the project is more likely to be driven by the needs of the industry rather than political agenda or personal profit. Additionally, these organizations attract subject-matter experts from across many sectors and industries.

Cyber Public-Private Partnerships must provide value to its partners.—These partnerships must understand and not be threatened by each other's agendas. Businesses need to understand that Governments are trying to solve complex problems while competing for limited resources. Government needs to understand that businesses can only participate in partnerships if they can afford to work at the rate at which the Government is willing or able to pay. The allure of an appointment or invitation to a Government partnership fades quickly when weighed against the responsibility of creating value for the shareholders.

Cyber Public-Private Partnership must reduce redundancy and capitalize on core competencies.—Participants in partnerships should be vetted for their expertise and ability to produce results. Competing interests and inclusion for any other reason than expertise is counterproductive to measurable results.

Cybersecurity public-private partnerships should capitalize on and use the most accurate data available.—Whenever possible, the creation of cybersecurity work force should directly correlate to the needs of the market. Partnerships should receive demand data directly from employers and match those needs to the programs and institutions that produce the required skills.

Cybersecurity Public-Private Partnership must be creative and disruptive when necessary.—The work force deficit in cybersecurity is showing little signs of getting better. Current methodologies are routinely failing to produce the required result through the traditional method of granting block funding to Government-subsidized higher education. This problem will only be solved with careful analysis, accurate data, and creative and disruptive ideas. Ideas such as allowing coding to be utilized to fulfill a foreign language credit in high school or offering incentives to cybersecurity professionals to purchase a house within a State's borders could produce unprecedented results if resources and political support are given.

Thank you for the opportunity to be here today and I look forward to answering any questions that you may have.

Mr. RATCLIFFE. Thank you, Mr. Rapp. The Chair now recognizes Mr. Jarvis for 5 minutes.

STATEMENT OF DAVID JARVIS, SECURITY AND CIO LEAD, IBM INSTITUTE FOR BUSINESS VALUE

Mr. JARVIS. Chairman Guthrie, Chairman Ratcliffe, Ranking Member Davis, Ranking Member Richmond, and distinguished Members, I am honored to appear before both committees today to discuss the insufficient supply of cybersecurity skills, to protect the economic and National security interests of the United States and the global digital infrastructure.

I work at IBM as part of the IBM Institute for Business Value, which explores research and reports on emerging business and technology issues, connecting our clients with leading practices. I primarily focus on cybersecurity and the various aspects surrounding the discipline.

To understand IBM's approach to skills and talent for cybersecurity, it is important to understand the people behind our security brand. We have roughly 8,000 subject-matter experts around the world. Since 2015, IBM security has hired nearly 2,000 into its security business. We must intelligently manage and struggle for scarce talent daily.

Simply put, cybersecurity professionals are not produced by the education system in the United States in the quantities or with the correct hard and soft skills needed. The education system is not aligned to produce a work force that can defend us from today's cybersecurity threats.

There are many estimates as to the size of the skills gap and how long it may take to close. While the size of the gap certainly indicates the severity of the problem, the bigger point is, unless we better align our education system with the core attributes and skills needed in cybersecurity, the Nation will continue to be at risk.

I would like to start by thanking you for your leadership with the House passing the Perkins Career and Technical Education Act twice. The recent letter signed by 59 Senators gives hope the Senate will soon act, as well. Thank you again for passing the bill which IBM believes will help students get the right education for today's jobs.

Second, IBM urges Congress to ease the pathway to jobs for new-collar workers. This involves tapping professionals who may not have a traditional college degree but have the necessary technical skills and aptitudes. To expand new-collar skills, IBM is pursuing and experimenting with a multitude of approaches activity the entire supply chain of talent. We are utilizing the new education model P–TECH. In the United States and other countries, P–TECH connects high school, college, and the world of work for historically disadvantaged populations. P–TECH starts with an employer committing to students that they will be first in line for a job if the school teaches them the core and technical skills needed.

The cornerstone for this program is industry partners articulating the skills needed to be taught. IBM security is currently partnering with programs specifically for cybersecurity in New York and Maryland. IBM seeks out military veterans who are by nature well aligned to cybersecurity positions. We recently announced we will hire 2,000 U.S. veterans over the next 4 years across our business. Veterans are a natural fit for a new-collar approach, bringing their skills and talents, but not necessarily formal degrees.

IBM is also driving education programs for middle and high schools. Our IBM Cyber Day for Girls events Nation-wide provide middle-school-aged girls with the opportunity to learn more about cybersecurity careers from female leaders in the field, reaching them at a critical age.

We are also partnering with community colleges to build the skills of the future through our community college skills accelerator. With growing numbers of community colleges offering cybersecurity programs, they are an increasingly important source of talent and they should be sufficiently supported and nurtured.

To address the different skill and education needs of new-collar workers, employers need to build a local cybersecurity ecosystem that provides a robust support program for new hires and supports on continuous learning and upscaling. Employers need to participate in regional partnerships with work force development programs, secondary schools, and technical and vocational schools. Examples of partnerships between employers and educators include joint cybersecurity curriculum committees, externships for local instructors to keep their skills fresh and relevant, the sponsorship of cyber teams, and programs with local middle/high-school students to generate interest in the field.

The Federal Government should adopt a new-collar approach to reach into expanded sources of labor. Federal agencies should explore the P–TECH model for work force development strategies that they can improper. By indicating what it takes to be first in line for a job, they can help address their own cybersecurity work force needs.

IBM believes new-collar workers can be an important component of the Nation's overall approach to tackling the cybersecurity skills gap. By not tapping into underutilized sources of talent across the country and supporting and nurturing it, we are doing a disservice to everyone and not securing ourselves as well as we could.

Finally, as Congress looks to reform the Higher Education Act, a good starting point is to eliminate existing regulatory obstacles imposed between individuals and cybersecurity careers. For example, work-based learning is a critical source of skills, particularly in cybersecurity. However, the Federal work-study program prohibits more than 25 percent of funds administered by a college or university from use off-campus for relevant internships or other work-based learning with private-sector employers.

Eliminating the restrictions would increase the flexibility of students and institutions of higher education. Thank you, Members of both committees, for the opportunity to present IBM's thoughts, strategies, and activities on improving cybersecurity education and your consideration of this testimony. Thank you.

[The prepared statement of Mr. Jarvis follows:]

PREPARED STATEMENT OF DAVID JARVIS

OCTOBER 24, 2017

Chairman Guthrie, Chairman Ratcliffe, Ranking Member Davis, Ranking Member Richmond, and distinguished Members, I am honored to appear before both committees today to discuss the insufficient supply of cybersecurity skills and the increased demand to fulfil important cybersecurity positions to protect the economic and National security interests of the United States and the global digital infrastructure.

In my testimony, I will describe the cyber threat landscape, the skills needed to protect against those threats, what IBM is doing to promote those skills including our "new-collar" approach, and finally, what the Government should do to improve the supply of cybersecurity skills and jobs.

To set the stage, I work at IBM as part of the Institute for Business Value, which explores and researches emerging business and technology issues impacting a variety of industries. We report insights from that research and provide practical guidance to the market and our clients. I primarily focus on cybersecurity and the various aspects surrounding the discipline—whether it be technical, societal, or economic.

Cybersecurity professionals are not produced by the education system in the United States in the quantities or skill levels needed. This is a problem that isn't going away anytime soon. However, with great challenges come creative solutions that many dedicated individuals and organizations are pursuing. At IBM, we believe that some cybersecurity jobs can be filled through a new-collar approach that involves tapping professionals who may not have a traditional college degree but do have the needed technical skills and aptitudes. This approach was outlined by our CEO, Ginni Rometty, at the end of 2016, as a way to address skills gaps across technology-related sectors.[1] By better aligning the education system with industry we can develop the skills needed to fight cyber crime, fill jobs, and reduce data breaches.

IBM'S SECURITY CAPABILITIES

IBM Security is the largest security vendor selling exclusively to enterprises. IBM manages 35 billion security events per day for our clients—one of the largest security intelligence operations in the world. IBM Security has 17,000 clients in 133 countries, 8,000 employees, including researchers, developers, and subject-matter experts focused on security, in 36 IBM Security locations around the globe. In sum, we "see" a lot in cyber space and have also dedicated over $2 billion in research and development to "out innovate" the cyber criminals.

To understand IBM Security, it's important to understand the people behind the brand. As part of the 8,000 subject-matter experts we have on board, IBM Security has:

- Researchers analyzing software for vulnerabilities.
- Incident Response teams (IBM X-Force IRIS) in the wake of a breach conducting forensic investigations and working with law enforcement.
- Interim CISOs that help organizations scale and address cybersecurity planning.
- Malware, spam, and Dark Web analysts, spending hours understanding the tactics criminals are using to target and infiltrate organizations.
- Security Intelligence analysts working in and deploying Security Operation Centers (SOCs) across the globe.

Since 2015, IBM Security has hired nearly 2,000 additional experts into its Security business, including world-class developers, consultants, and research professionals.

Additionally, IBM Security is developing and using cognitive cybersecurity systems like Watson to augment the skills and capabilities of security teams. With the ability to interpret huge volumes of structured and unstructured data, staff with cognitive tools can better reveal patterns and put security events in context. Using data mining, machine learning, natural language processing, and human computer interaction, cognitive systems provide evidence-based recommendations to help cybersecurity experts act with confidence, at speed and scale.

TODAY'S SECURITY THREATS

Today, just about all the breaches we hear and read about involves the exfiltration of data. A cyber criminal breaks into a system, gets access to information, downloads that data, and extorts it for profit or influence.

The IBM X-Force Threat Intelligence Index 2017 found in 2016 more than 4 billion records were leaked, more than the combined total from the two previous years, redefining the meaning of the term "mega breach." In one case, a single source leaked more than 1.5 billion records. The industries experiencing the highest number of incidents and reported records breached were information and communica-

---

[1] *https://www.usatoday.com/story/tech/news/2016/12/13/ibms-rometty-talk-new-collar-jobs-trump/95370718/.*

tions, Government, and financial services. Mega breaches have continued to penetrate all sectors with unabated threats in 2017.[2]

Additionally, late last year IBM and the Ponemon Institute unveiled the results of the annual Cyber Resilient Organization study, which found businesses are continuing to fail when it comes to preparing for and responding to cyber attacks. Companies are being attacked successfully more frequently, they cannot keep business operations going effectively or recover quickly, and most have not done adequate planning or preparation for an incident.[3] Considering the vast digital dependencies for organizations, it is no longer a matter of "if" but a matter of "when" an incident will happen.

We are seeing security attacks and techniques continue to evolve across skill level, geography, and sectors. It is now estimated to be one of the largest illegal economies in the world, costing the global economy more than $445 billion dollars a year.[4] To put this in perspective, $445 billion is greater than the GDP of more than 160 different countries, including Ireland, Malaysia, Finland, Denmark, and Portugal, among many others.

The most sophisticated thieves operate like a well-oiled global business. They build development tools and collaborate on software. They share knowledge about targets and vulnerabilities. They recruit, educate, promote, and reward their work force. In fact, each successful attack proliferates the skills, tools, and ecosystem because hackers often reuse malware and other vulnerabilities that they know are proven to work. Think of it as on-the-job education.

As the threat emanates from a variety of angles, we need to respond with innovative cyber defenses including a work force with a diverse set of skills that are constantly updated. Persistent and well-funded cyber crime organizations are constantly probing a range of vulnerabilities. They look for simple misconfigurations of installed software, but also have the capability to carry out sophisticated brute force, phishing, and malware conflicts. The spread of attacks from simple to complex requires a broad set of skills and capabilities to respond—across skill levels, information technology defenses, organizations, and geographies.

Due to the current lack of skills, cyber crime creates chronic infections of Government, enterprise, and individual systems that take months (if not years) to heal, and are corrosive to the economy and public trust.

THE SKILLS CHALLENGE AND NEEDED CAPABILITIES TO DEFEND AGAINST CYBER THREATS

An organization is only as good as the people that are part of it. The challenge of recruiting and retaining the best technical and business professionals is a constant worry for any organization, even more so in the cybersecurity field.

The cybersecurity talent issue isn't limited to a few sectors; it runs across the board from Government to education to health care and all industries. Strong talent is needed in all communities from rural farms that increasing rely on information technology to financial service companies in large urban areas.

There are many estimates as to the size of the shortage of cybersecurity professionals. Frost & Sullivan predicts that the growing gap between available qualified cybersecurity professionals and unfulfilled positions will reach 1.8 million by 2022.[5] While the size of the gap certainly indicates the severity of the problem, the bigger point is that unless we change and improve our approach dramatically, the gap will be an elusive thing to catch up to and close.

Many leaders believe that not enough is being done about the shortage. According to a report by the Center for Strategic and International Studies and Intel Security, three out of four security professionals surveyed believe their Government is not investing enough in cybersecurity talent.[6]

The inherent complexities that make cybersecurity challenging have created this severe skills shortage. Even though Government, industry, and education are attempting to address the problem through many different initiatives, the entire supply chain of talent is stressed. Industry is facing a shortage of qualified candidates

---

[2] *https://www.ibm.com/security/xforce/research.html.*

[3] "The 2016 Cyber Resilient Organization", Ponemon Institute and IBM, November 2016.

[4] Net Losses: Estimating the Global Cost of Cyber Crime, Center for Strategic and International Studies, June 2014.

[5] "The 2017 Global Information Security Workforce Study: Women in Cybersecurity." Frost & Sullivan. March 2017. *https://iamcybersafe.org/wp-content/uploads/2017/03/WomensReport.pdf.*

[6] "Hacking the Skills Shortage: A study of the international shortage in cybersecurity skills." Center for Strategic and International Studies and Intel Security. 2016. *https://www.mcafee.com/ca/resources/reports/.*

with the necessary hands-on skills and product experience. Those working as security professionals today are under constant pressure, as they need continuous education and professional development to keep up with evolving technologies and the threat landscape. They are also challenged to find time to properly mentor and educate new hires.

Academic institutions want to meet industry needs, but they are struggling to evolve and develop curriculum to keep pace with industry shifts and technological advances. There is also a shortage of qualified teachers and professors at both the university and community college levels, as many are lured away to industry by competitive salaries. Finally, students interested in pursuing the cybersecurity field are faced with defining their own career path from a myriad of options and then obtain the significant education and experience required.

At the most basic level, employers must ensure that software, networks, and cyber defenses are correctly installed and configured. Skills for these broadly-needed services are low to middle but required throughout the economy in large numbers.

At the other extreme, chief information security officers (CISOs) for large enterprises and Government agencies are required to orchestrate a broad set of defensive capabilities and respond to a bewildering array of breaches. CISOs are highly-skilled positions with significant education and experience who must balance managing their own security operations with advising, guiding, and educating their C-suites and boards of directors.

What skills should new cybersecurity professionals focus on? No matter the educational background of the professional, there are some essential elements. These elements can be classified into two groups: Core attributes and skills.

Core attributes can be considered a general disposition beneficial to security professionals—a set of common personality traits and learned behaviors. This includes being investigative, methodical, analytical, ethical, reliable, constantly learning, a good communicator, and able to team with others to solve challenging problems. Skills include both technical and workplace-related abilities. A new security professional may not have all these skills at first, but focusing on them over time will provide greater career path flexibility and the foundation for technical or business-focused security leadership positions.

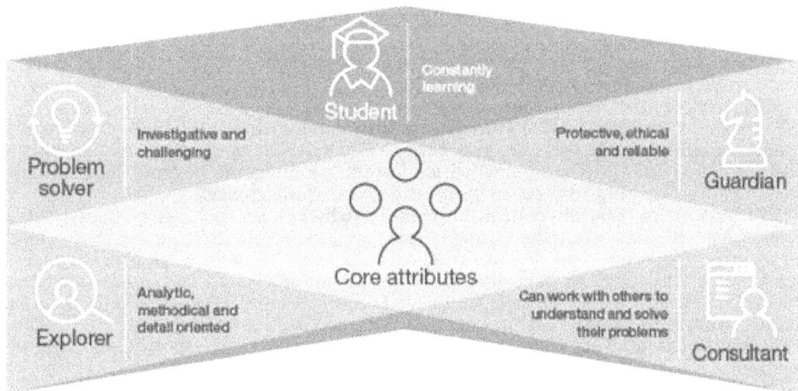

DEVELOPING CYBERSECURITY SKILLS: THE IBM NEW-COLLAR APPROACH

IBM's new-collar approach focuses on skills—not degrees earned—and emphasizes work-based learning and core skills like teaming and adaptability.

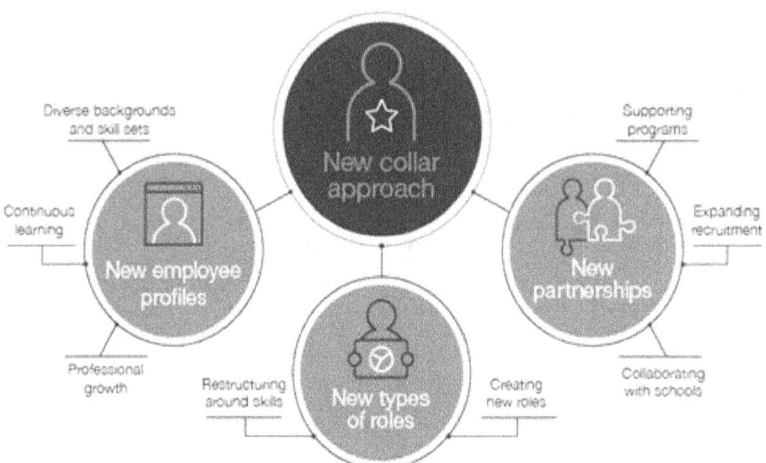

The cornerstone of a new-collar approach and a major component of the overall strategy necessary to address the cybersecurity skills gap is to seek new sources of skills that may not have been pursued in the past, due to a lack of traditional academic credentials.

A new-collar approach is used at IBM to fill both technical and non-technical jobs. We have identified some specific cybersecurity jobs as suitable places to start. This includes "builders" such as integration engineers and cybersecurity developers, "operators" such as threat monitoring analysts and security operations center analysts, and "communicators" such as technical writers and security awareness educators.

A new-collar approach focuses on skills—not degrees earned—as a prerequisite to find and attract nontraditional candidates with diverse backgrounds and skill sets. Once hired, these new employees are expected to strive for continuous learning and professional growth. A new-collar approach recognizes there are alternative ways to learn the skills needed. For example, respondents from a CSIS and Intel Security study ranked hands-on experience and professional certifications as better ways to acquire cybersecurity skills than a degree.[7]

To expand new-collar skills, IBM is experimenting with a multitude of approaches to educate and develop the next generation of cybersecurity professionals. These include creating and developing new education programs, going beyond the traditional classroom and making new connections and sharing information.

IBM is utilizing the new education model Pathways in Technology Early College High School (P–TECH) in the United States and other countries specifically for cybersecurity. Currently, we are working with Excelsior Academy at Newburgh Free Academy in New York (a partnership between the Newburgh Enlarged City School District, IBM, and SUNY Orange Community College) and P–TECH@Carver in Baltimore, Maryland (a partnership between Carver Vocational Technical High School, IBM, and Baltimore City Community College) on cybersecurity-specific pathway programs.

The P–TECH model of schools has four key elements:
- Alignment of the Program of Study for grades 9–14 with the skills needed by an employer.
- Mentors for all students from the employer.
- Internships for students from the employer.
- A commitment that graduating students will be first in line for a job with the employer.

P–TECH model could be adopted by Federal agencies to create job opportunities for students, and as an approach for their work force needs. Over 60 P–TECH schools exist throughout the United States including in my home State of Rhode Island and there are many more on the way.

---

[7] "Hacking the Skills Shortage: A study of the international shortage in cybersecurity skills." Center for Strategic and International Studies and Intel Security. 2016. *https:// www.mcafee.com/ca/resources/reports/rp-hacking-skills-shortage.pdf*

We are partnering with community colleges to build the skills of the future through our Community College Skills Accelerator. This program provides access to documented skills roadmaps, access to free IBM tools, including platforms, services, and software, access to IBM mentorship and subject-matter expertise, including collaboration on curriculum review and creation and pathways to employment, including internships and apprenticeships.

With growing numbers offering cybersecurity programs, community colleges are an important source of talent. However, fewer than 30 percent of the roughly 1,100 public and independent community colleges across the United States offer a cybersecurity degree, certificate, or course.[8] Those that offer cybersecurity classes have difficulty updating the content and finding the needed teaching staff. The additional demands of accreditation, distributional requirements, and financial aid requirements make cybersecurity education very challenging for educators.

Programs like the National Security Agency and the Department of Homeland Security sponsored National Centers of Academic Excellence and the National Science Foundation's Advanced Technological Education program that supports regional cybersecurity programs at 2-year colleges, are very important resources for these community college programs.

IBM is also driving education programs for middle and high schools. This includes an initiative with ISECOM, a non-profit organization which produces the Hacker High School project—open cybersecurity courses designed specifically for teenagers to develop critical thinking and hands-on, technical skills. As part of this collaboration, IBM is providing sponsorship, expert guidance, and IBM Security tools for new Hacker High School lessons focused on the skills needed for an entry-level security operation center (SOC) analyst—a position that is in demand. IBM also hosts "Cyber Day for Girls" events Nation-wide to provide middle school-aged girls with the opportunity to learn more about cybersecurity careers, reaching them at a critical age.

IBM partners with hundreds of universities and colleges world-wide to develop the next generation of cyber talent. Through our Academic Initiative program, we provide access to skills and software at no charge. We also sponsor and recruit at key university cyber-competitions, including ones at the Rochester Institute of Technology, New York University, and the National Collegiate Cyber Defense Competition.

Military veterans bring unique talents, mindset, and skills that are attractive to the technology industry, and even more so to cybersecurity positions. The mission focus mentality and professionalism are attributes needed to protect and defend networks. IBM recently announced it will hire 2,000 U.S. veterans over the next 4 years as part of the company's broader pledge to hire 25,000 workers by 2020. Veterans are a natural fit for the new-collar approach. We developed the IBM Veterans Employment Accelerator to focus on education and certification programs for military veterans and participate in Veteran recruiting events and transition summits.[9]

Women are globally underrepresented in the cybersecurity profession at 11 percent, much lower than the representation of women in the overall global work force. In 2016, women in cybersecurity earned less than men at every level.[10] IBM is actively recruiting underrepresented groups through conferences and organizations like the International Consortium of Minority Cybersecurity Professionals (ICMCP), the Grace Hopper Celebration and Women in CyberSecurity (WiCyS).[11] Additionally, we have an internal network called Women in Security Excelling (WISE), an IBM professional development group that also sponsors external events like the "Cyber Day for Girls" programs in middle schools and provides scholarships to attend security conferences.[12]

IBM's efforts to build a cybersecurity work force prove to be working—as mentioned, we have built a business of over 8,000 experts including an additional 2,000 since 2015—although job openings at IBM Security are still plentiful. That work

---

[8] "2016 Fact Sheet." American Association of Community Colleges. *http://www.aacc.nche.edu/AboutCC/Documents/AACCFactSheetsR2.pdf*; IBM Institute for Business Value interview with Casey O'Brien, Executive Director & Principal Investigator, National CyberWatch Center. February 21, 2017.

[9] "Citizen IBM Blog—Veterans Employment Accelerator." IBM website, accessed March 19, 2017. *https://www.ibm.com/blogs/citizen-ibm/tag/ibm-veterans-employment-accelerator.*

[10] *https://iamcybersafe.org/wp-content/uploads/2017/03/WomensReport.pdf.*

[11] International Consortium of Minority Cybersecurity Professionals website, accessed April 3, 2017. *https://icmcp.org/*; Women in CyberSecurity website, accessed April 3, 2017 *https://www.csc.tntech.edu/wicys/.*

[12] "How IBM Supports Women Building their Careers in Cyber Security." IBM Jobs Blog, November 7, 2016 *https://blog.ibm.jobs/2016/11/07/how-ibm-supports-women-building-their-careers-in-cyber-security/.*

force is a result of reaching new sources through our new-collar recruitment—in fact, nearly 20 percent of our security hires since 2015 have fit into this "new-collar" category.

Our success provides some guidance to efforts to create policies around building a cybersecurity work force, but in many ways, is dependent on the willingness to address the overall challenges in the education system.

WHAT SHOULD THE GOVERNMENT DO TO ADDRESS CYBERSECURITY SKILLS AND CAPABILITIES?

IBM urges the committees to examine four areas for changed Government activity that will improve the cybersecurity work force. Those four areas are listed below and then discussed in more detail:

- *Reauthorize Perkins CTE.*—The Government needs to improve the alignment between the education system and the skills needed for today's jobs through re-authorization of the Perkins Career and Technical Education Act and the Higher Education Act.
- *Explore P–TECH Model.*—Federal agencies should explore the P–TECH model for work force development strategies they can implement.
- *Remove Obstacles to Cybersecurity Skills.*—Broad reforms to higher education appear necessary due to poor performance on inclusion, graduation rates, defaults, and alignment with today's jobs. A good starting point is to eliminate existing regulatory obstacles imposed between individuals and cybersecurity careers.
- *Expand New-Collar Hiring.*—The Federal Government should adopt a new-collar approach to reach and expand sources of labor.

Alignment through Reauthorization of Perkins Career and Technical Education.—The education system is poorly connected to the job market. Schools and colleges often do not offer students relevant classes in emerging areas such as cybersecurity and do not emphasize core attributes like teaming and communication in a program of study. Aligning the education system with the skills needed for today's jobs would more effectively spend Federal dollars to help our Nation's students acquire the skills that they need and employers are demanding.

Recently, the House passed a reauthorization of the Perkins Career and Technical Education Act. Although the Senate has failed to take up the legislation, recently 59 Senators sent a letter to the Chair and Ranking Member of the Senate HELP Committee urging action. The letter called for:

- Align CTE programs to the needs of the regional, State, and local labor market;
- Support effective and meaningful collaboration between secondary and post-secondary institutions and employers;
- Increase student participation in work-based learning opportunities; and
- Promote the use of industry-recognized credentials and other recognized post-secondary credentials.

IBM urges the Senate to move forward on reauthorization of the Perkins Career and Technical Education Act, and to incorporate these principles into its reauthorization of the Higher Education Act.

Explore P–TECH Model Participation by Federal Agencies.—The P–TECH model is based on a collaboration between employers and educators to improve alignment of the existing education system with needed job skills. Developing programs of study and educational materials is the responsibility of our Nation's educators, but P–TECH employers play a vital role by telling what skills are necessary "to be first in line for a job". Defining skills needs, providing mentors, internships, and committing that graduates will be "first in line for a job" are all employer responsibilities in the P–TECH model.

Federal agencies are major employers and should explore the work force development strategies developed and tested by the private sector through the P–TECH model schools. Federal agencies could join other P–TECH employers that provide information to work force boards and educators on needed job skills. Federal agencies could provide work-based learning opportunities including mentors and internships. Both student and potential Federal employers benefit from enhancing skills learned through improved alignment and work-based learning.

Eliminate Obstacles on the Critical Pathway to Cybersecurity Skills.—The education system has appalling key performance metrics in areas relevant to cybersecurity work force development—first-generation entrants into higher education are scarce, completion rates are low, misalignment of skills and jobs is high, and default rates on student loans are astronomical.

Adopting the critical pathway approach used in health care to improve quality can help improve the cybersecurity work force by highlighting the most problematic steps in the education process.

For example, work-based learning is a critical source of skills—particularly in cybersecurity. However, the Federal work-study program prohibits more than 25 percent of funds administered by a college or university from use for off-campus for relevant internships or other work-based learning with private-sector employers.

Eliminating the restrictions would increase the flexibility of students and institutions of higher education to use their Federal work study allocations for part- and full-time off-campus cooperative education and other work-study purposes. Rather than forcing work-study grants to be used for dining hall jobs, students could get internships that were relevant to their majors and provided critical work experience and skills.

IBM urges Congress to return flexibility to students and higher-education institutions in their use of work-study funds.

New-Collar Approaches.—Finally, IBM recommends that organizations expand their recruitment of the new-collar cybersecurity work force. For a more robust new-collar approach, employers need to create new-collar career pathways in their work force strategy with five components:

- Skill Maps
- Broader Recruitment
- Education Ecosystem
- Work-based Learning
- Retention

Document the skills and experience that are essential today and in the future. Use that skill map to help design clear career paths for security functions, focusing on what skills are needed in different cybersecurity roles at each level. In recruiting, substitute the skill map for degrees as prerequisites. The skill map should determine when academic degrees are included in hiring requirements. Do all security hires really need 4-year university degrees? Do not miss a potential star by imposing arbitrary degree requirements before job candidates they get a chance to prove themselves—realize that skills and experience can come from a variety of places.

Recruit new-collar workers from sources beyond traditional higher-education sources. Seek students who are earning cybersecurity certificates, AAS, and Associate degrees at community colleges; don't limit efforts to a select set of 4-year and research universities. As mentioned earlier, veterans and separating service personnel are another new-collar work force that has critical skill attributes such as leadership, teaming, and adaptability. IBM has specific recruitment programs for veterans and separating armed services personnel that allow their skills to be mapped against IBM job roles.

To address the different skill and education needs of new-collar workers, employers need to build a local cybersecurity ecosystem that provides a robust support program for new hires and focuses on continuous learning and upskilling. Employers need to participate in regional partnerships—with work force development organizations, secondary schools, and technical and vocational schools. Examples of partnerships between employers and educators include joint cybersecurity curriculum committees, externships for local instructors to keep their skills fresh and relevant, the sponsorship of cyber teams, and programs with local middle and high schools to generate interest in the field. These groups are always looking for subject-matter experts and mentors that employers can provide to improve the cybersecurity pipeline.

Work-based learning and "earn and learn" strategies are critical for new-collar career pathways. Employ techniques like mentorships, internships, rotational assignments, shadowing, and other opportunities for new cybersecurity hires to gain experience and learn. Allow them to explore their options and opportunities—not everyone knows what they want to do right away.

With an expanded recruiting aperture bringing new talent in, there must be comparable efforts to work to retain the talent. Keep employees engaged by providing opportunities for them to advance and keep skills up-to-date through classes, certifications, conferences. Cybersecurity is a highly dynamic field, which requires a constant refreshing of skills. Additionally, support existing new-collar employees from other functions who want to move into cybersecurity as a new career.

CONCLUSION

With the five approaches above, IBM believes new-collar workers can add an important component of the Nation's overall approach to tackling the cybersecurity skills gap. It is applicable across industry and Government and has tangible benefits for both employers and potential employees. By not tapping into underutilized sources of talent across the country and supporting and nurturing it, we are doing a disservice to everyone and not securing ourselves as well as we could. There are many innovative approaches to improving cybersecurity education happening all across the country, but to truly address the cybersecurity skills gap we need to scale these approaches, including new-collar ones.

Thank you Members of both committees for the opportunity to present IBM's thoughts, strategy, and activities on improving cybersecurity education and your consideration of this testimony.

Mr. RATCLIFFE. Thank you, Mr. Jarvis. Chair now recognizes Dr. Ralls for 5 minutes.

STATEMENT OF R. SCOTT RALLS, PRESIDENT, NORTHERN VIRGINIA COMMUNITY COLLEGE

Mr. RALLS. Thank you, Chairman Ratcliffe, Chairman Guthrie, Chairman Richmond and Davis, and Members of the committee. Thank you for the population to testify the afternoon.

The road to economic recovery from the Great Recession has run right through the middle of America's community colleges. As we emerge into a new era of net job growth, community colleges again stand at the forefront in addressing talent and skills gaps. Because we are overrepresented by students from first-generation, low-income, and minority backgrounds, community colleges are uniquely situated to provide a gateway to economic opportunity that must draw—for fields like cybersecurity that must draw from a wider population to address overall talent gaps.

An era where these gaps are keenly felt is the field of cybersecurity, a skill set where jobs are growing three times faster than for IT jobs in general, which are growing at a rate much faster than other occupational areas. In the greater Washington region, where my college is located, cybersecurity job postings have grown 74 percent since 2014, and we have had the most new job postings over the past year—more than twice as many as any region of the country for the past year.

Filling this gap, meeting this challenge, and in turn providing a great economic opportunity for our students is our most pressing work force priority. Consequently, we are not just pursuing a unidimensional strategy, but moving simultaneously down multiple fronts. These include scaling. Four years ago, as was mentioned, we grew a cybersecurity certificate program into a separate applied associate's degree, growing from an initial 50 students to approximately 1,500 today. We were one of the early certified academic excellence programs with the National Security Agency, and today we share our experience with other colleges as one of four National resource centers.

Ours is a practical program that emphasizes application, certifications, and participation in meaningful competition. We are constantly looking for ways to scale to meet our growth challenges by hiring new faculty, pursuing opportunities to endow faculty to overcome the gap between what is top faculty pay and average industry pay, and leasing, purchasing, and renovating multiple facilities.

We articulate—which means that we seamlessly connect to eight senior higher education partners so students can complete a bachelor's degree, which is typically a minimal requirement for cybersecurity employment. At two of our six campuses, students can complete their bachelor's degree on-site, including at our new regional work force center in Woodbridge, which houses our cyber range and our on-site degree completion program with George Washington University.

We aggressively draw from the rich talent pool of transitioning military veterans at our college and in our community. We have partnered closely with Marine Corps University to provide concentrated surge educational opportunities, developed a unique technology boot camp for veterans called Uncommon Coders, articulated military occupational specialty credit into our cyber degree program, and worked with our State legislators to gain the ability to charge lower tuition rates for our active-duty military in these programs.

We reach into high schools, underserved communities, and untapped populations. We have a team called sySTEMic that specifically reaches into public schools to provide STEM outreach, including cyber, where we partner with Northrop Grumman, who helps us to fund and support training high school educators who can provide instruction and dual enrollment through our programs.

We have a very unique, complementary, and mutually beneficial partnership with the great work force development agency Year Up, who recruits, develops internship opportunities, financially supports students who are enrolled in our cyber and IT programs. This year, we have dedicated all of our Federal Perkins funding to draw female students through our cyber and IT programs.

Because as you have heard, the cyber work force population is only 11 percent female, 12 percent minority. To meet the skills gap, that has to increase.

Now, quickly in moving on, we apprentice and aggressively seek out internship opportunities with our cyber students. We do this through Year Up, with special employer relationships like we have with the U.S. Senate Sergeant-at-Arms, also a special new relationship with Amazon Web Services, where we support and sponsored the first AWS apprenticeship program for the hardest-to-fill jobs that are out there right now in cloud security.

We certify with the assistance of our unique Virginia Fast Forward program, which is the first performance-funded work force certification program in the Nation. It allows us to provide valuable certifications in areas like CompTIA Security+, Certified Ethical Hacker, at only one-third of the actual cost. Cybersecurity job postings typically require certifications more so than IT in general.

Finally, key to all this is working very aggressively to learn and seek feedback and react to the information we receive from our valuable employer community, our rich cybersecurity employers in our region. A secret weapon for us is the Northern Virginia Technology Council, which is the largest employer group of its type in the Nation. We are very proud to be their first academic partner and with them sponsored the skills talent assessment for our region just last year.

In sum, we are taking a multi-faceted approach to address the cybersecurity work force challenge in our region. We do so not only because it meets the needs of our employers, but most importantly it provides such great opportunity for our students. Last year, our college was recognized by the research of Stanford economist Raj Chetty as having one of the highest percentages of students who grew up in the bottom 20 percent of income but emerged into the top 20 percent as adults after attending a college such as ours.

We are very fortunate to support a region where the economic opportunities which include cybersecurity job opportunities make that possible. We are also humbled to be an institution that provides that educational ladder to help students of all backgrounds to be able to grasp those opportunities. Thank you.

[The prepared statement of Dr. Ralls follows:]

PREPARED STATEMENT OF R. SCOTT RALLS

OCTOBER 23, 2017

To the Chairs and Members of the committees: Thank you for the opportunity to testify this afternoon.

The road to economic recovery from the Great Recession ran through the middle of America's community colleges, and as we emerge into a new era of net job growth, community colleges are again at the forefront in addressing talent and skills gaps. We are positioned to serve students from lower income, first generation, and minority backgrounds. Accordingly, we are uniquely capable of providing a gateway to economic opportunity and careers that must attract a wider population to fill job needs.

An area where these needs are keenly felt is in the field of cybersecurity. Information technology jobs are growing at a rate much faster than most other occupational areas. Faster still is the growth in jobs in cybersecurity, a field growing three times more rapidly than information technology jobs in general.

My name is Scott Ralls and I am president of Northern Virginia Community College, or NOVA as we are known in the region we serve, a region which has the highest concentration of cybersecurity jobs in the United States. In the greater Washington region, cybersecurity job postings have grown 74% since 2014. Our area has more than twice as many overall new job postings than any other area in the country.

Filling this gap and meeting this challenge is an economic opportunity for the students at our college. Last year, our college was ranked in the social mobility research of Stanford economist Raj Chetty, as having one of the highest percentages of students who grew up in the bottom 20% of income brackets as children, but emerged in the top 20% of income earners as adults. We are very fortunate to serve a region that has the economic opportunities to make that possible. We are humbled to be the institution providing the educational ladder to help our students get there.

Taking this challenge on requires more than a one-dimensional program approach. It requires that we pursue a multi-faceted strategy that includes:

Scaling.—Four years ago we grew a cybersecurity certificate program into a separate, applied associates degree, and have expanded the program from an initial 50 students to nearly 1,500 today. We began as one of the early Certified Academic Excellence programs with the National Security Agency. Today we share our experience with and guide other colleges as one of four National rsource centers. Ours is a practical, work force-focused program that emphasizes application, acquisition of certifications, and participation in meaningful competition. To meet the challenges of growth we are hiring new faculty. To overcome the gap between top community college faculty pay and average industry pay, we announced the first-ever endowed chair in the State community college system and are pursuing other opportunities to attract top talent. To meet our capital needs we are leasing, purchasing, and renovating multiple facilities.

We articulate, meaning that we seamlessly connect to nine great university partners so students can complete a bachelosr degree. This is important as it is typically a minimum requirement for employment in cybersecurity with Federal agencies and contractors. At two of our six campuses, students can complete their bachelor degree on-site including at our new Regional Workforce Center in Woodbridge. This center houses our cyber range and the on-site completion program with George Washington University.

We aggressively draw from the rich talent pool of transitioning military and Veterans at our college and within our community. Currently active-duty service members and veterans make up 15% of our student body. Four years ago, we partnered with the United States Marine Corps and Marine Corps University to provide concentrated "surge" educational opportunities. We have developed a unique technology boot camp for Veterans called Uncommon Coders and worked with our State legislators to offer our courses at a discount to service members around the globe. We have made it possible for Marines with technology-related military occupational specialties to receive up to 23 credit hours upon entering our cyber program.

We reach into high schools, underserved communities, and untapped populations. We have a team called SySTEMic that specifically connects with local schools to provide STEM hands-on STEM experiences, including experiential learning in cybersecurity. With a generous grant from Northrup Grumman, we partner with school systems to certify instructors to become NOVA adjunct faculty delivering dual enrollment cybersecurity programs directly in our high schools. We have a unique and mutually beneficial partnership with the Nationally-recognized work force development organization, Year Up. Year Up recruits, develops internship opportunities, financially supports and provides supplemental education to underprivileged youth enrolled in our IT and cyber programs. And this year, we have dedicated all of our Federal CTE/Perkins funding to efforts to attract female students into information technology and cybersecurity fields. We recognize that the best opportunity to grow the cybersecurity work force is to address the underrepresentation of minorities and women in the cyber work force. Specifically, the cybersecurity work force is reported to be only 11% female and 12% minority. By launching a new awareness campaign highlighting successful local women in IT and cyber and by providing new summer camps and clearer education pathways we hope to move the needle on retaining more women in the critical needs area.

In addition, we aggressively seek apprenticeship and internship opportunities for our cyber students. We create these opportunities through our Year Up collaboration and special partnerships we have made with multiple groups. To help meet the need for cloud security talent, judged to be the most difficult skillset for employers to find today, we recently initiated a partnership with our local Workforce Board, Apprenti, and Amazon Web Services to create Amazon Web Services' first East Coast apprenticeship program. This consists of a Veterans Associate Cloud Consultant Apprenticeship Program and a new Incumbent Cloud Support Associate Apprentice program to assist fulfillment and data center employees moving into technology opportunities. At its core, this is a program to move current Amazon employees into higher paying positions that Amazon could not otherwise fill.

We certify. Recently our State launched *Virginia Fast Forward Program*, the first performance-funded work force certification program in the Nation. This enables us to provide education and certifications such as COMPTIA Security+ and Certified Ethical Hacker at only a third of the market cost. This is key to job opportunity in cyber, as cybersecurity job postings are more likely to require certifications than information technology jobs in general.

Finally, and key to supporting all of our efforts, we aggressively learn and seek feedback from the cybersecurity employers in our region. A vital resource for us is the Northern Virginia Technology Council, the largest employer group of its type in the Nation. We are honored to be their first academic partner. Last year, we collaborated with NVTC to conduct the Greater Washington Technology Needs Assessment. This assessment identified cybersecurity skills as the second-most in demand technical skill in our region behind only computer programming skills.

We are taking a multi-faceted strategy to address the cybersecurity work force challenge in our region. We do so not only because it meets employer needs, but most importantly, it helps our students understand the needs of northern Virginia employers like General Dynamics, Booz Allen, and CACI. But to solve this problem requires an even deeper engagement between industry, education, and State and Federal partners all working toward a common goal of increase awareness, making cyber pathways clear and easy to navigate and providing work-learn opportunities in greater numbers.

Mr. RATCLIFFE. Thank you, Dr. Ralls, and thanks again to all of our witnesses today for your testimoneys. I now recognize myself for 5 minutes of questions.

Dr. Cambone, I want to start with you. First of all, do you agree with the premise that the cyber skills gap is getting worse? If so, with so much focus in recent years about expanding cyber educational opportunities, why do you think that is the case?

Mr. CAMBONE. Yes, the gap is growing. Second, in part, the difficulty I believe is not just with the number of students we have coming through the system, but the number of qualified faculty to teach, reaching back into high schools and even into grade schools. So as a way of addressing that, our cybersecurity center is actually holding what amounts to boot camps for high school teachers to try to begin to teach them the essentials.

Mr. RATCLIFFE. So let's set aside for a second displaced workers and others that can really help build and allow us to develop a cyber work force and focus on the kind of students that go to Texas A&M or some of the other universities. Is there any type of private-sector involvement in setting the cybersecurity courses that Texas A&M offers? Are there specific skill needs that either the private sector or the Government is telling you that need to be addressed?

Mr. CAMBONE. Yes to both. We are fairly tightly coupled with our colleagues over at NSA who have taken in over 20 students over the last 3 years in direct response to their demand pull, if you will. On the private side, as an example, we were told two semesters ago that we needed to do more secure coding.

For an institution of our size, we turned around a secure coding course in the following spring. So, yes, there is a feedback loop. I will be with our academic advisory committee, which is mostly private sector, Friday afternoon for just this purpose.

Mr. RATCLIFFE. So that sort-of leads into the question I had for Mr. Rapp. With respect to the cyber leadership alliance, does it play any role, can it play any role in advising—be a matchmaker, if you will, between businesses and schools?

Mr. RAPP. Absolutely. We work very closely with Purdue University and a new program that they have called CAREER Makers. Right now, we are submitting a proposal with several private companies to actually place a CAREER Makers in an underserved community in downtown Indianapolis. The Cyber Leadership Alliance with take that information directly from the employers and play matchmaker with the cohorts of students that are in Purdue and the other universities, such as Ivy Tech and Indiana University. So absolutely, that is primarily our function.

Mr. RATCLIFFE. Mr. Jarvis, let me shift to you. IBM is a very large company. How does IBM go about finding and recruiting cyber workers that may not have, say, a traditional educational background, a bachelor's degree or relevant certifications?

Mr. JARVIS. Sure, sure. So, I mean, obviously, traditionally, you know, we partner with and work with hundreds of universities around the world to get our talent globally. But when you look at kind-of these new sources, these, you know, new-collar workers, as well, this recently just—we just basically recently announced this earlier in the year, but, you know, we are beginning to work more with community colleges. We recruit at a lot of different security conferences and organizations, whether it is women in cybersecurity or the ICMCP, as well, that Mr. Richmond talked about before.

So, I mean, it is basically with those partnerships kind-of building our skills, building our talent pipeline, and with P–TECH, as well. I mean, we are trying to address the issue really at all elements of the game from high school all the way through community college through veterans programs, if we are recruiting at military bases, things like that. Those are all standard things that we typically do. We are looking to expand to do more, as well.

Mr. RATCLIFFE. Terrific. So there are a lot of folks that are going to ask a lot of questions today, but the bottom line I think for a lot of us is, you know, exactly how does the Government and the private sector best create an environment to incentivize both traditional students, and displaced workers, to make a career in cybersecurity? What as Members of Congress can we do to facilitate that? Very quickly, let me start left to right and give you all a chance to answer.

Mr. CAMBONE. Well, sir, it is a combination of funding always. But in this case, I don't think it is merely dollars. I think we have really got to extend from the universities backward into the high schools. We have to look after the education of the next cohort of educators. So we need to focus, as well, on students who are going to go on to take their PhDs so that they, in turn, can do the teaching we are going to need.

Mr. RATCLIFFE. Very quickly, Mr. Rapp, anything you want to add to that?

Mr. RAPP. I just think that we need to reduce some barriers, relook at OPM's requirements for hiring cybersecurity professionals, and where they fall on the GS level to increase that, security clearances and nationality issues.

Mr. RATCLIFFE. Terrific. Mr. Jarvis.

Mr. JARVIS. Yes, just in addition to what I said in my testimony, I think those are the primary things. But really, we are looking for just better alignment between the education system and the demands that we have.

Mr. RATCLIFFE. Terrific. Finally, Dr. Ralls, give you a quick chance to weigh in on that.

Mr. RALLS. We have benefited greatly from the NSA programs, the CIE programs, also the National Science Foundation Cyber Watch, which is at Montgomery College. Just as we have to scale to meet needs, those programs have to scale, as well, to meet our needs to be able to provide the training and education that is needed.

Mr. RATCLIFFE. Terrific. Chair now recognizes my friend from Louisiana, Mr. Richmond.

Mr. RICHMOND. Let me start with Dr. Ralls and Mr. Cambone. Let me just start with a basic question. Because you all deal with students, when they come out, is the private sector or public sector more attractive for them to go to? I would assume it is the private sector.

Mr. CAMBONE. Yes, sir.

Mr. RALLS. Our students are interested in jobs wherever they are. They also know that when they go into one area, public or private, they are going to have opportunities both ways because of the demand that is out there. So I don't see them really picking and choosing too much in that regard. They are interested in getting their foot in the door.

Mr. RICHMOND. Well, my experience with the people with the skills in cyber really have a choice where they want to go, because of the demand. Government is so rigid—I mean, we still operate with this, you know, traditional office setting-type area, and if you go to a lot of the private-sector companies that are employing cyber professionals, they have a different workplace and workspace.

So the question is, what can we do as Government to make Government more attractive for people coming out of school? So one idea would be, could you—could we become the industry standard in terms of offering continuing education or other ways for them to boost their skills while working for the Federal Government? What incentives can we give them to make the Federal Government more attractive, besides money, if you are telling me we are going to have a shortage of in-between 1.4 million and 1.8 million?

Mr. CAMBONE. Right. So the civil service arrangements, as you point out, are Teddy Roosevelt in their origins. They need to be updated. Among the things that we ought to take a look at is the career progression. These students, the people coming into the work force are not going to stay in a job for more than 5 years. While they are in that job, they need to be given important and interesting things to do.

If there is added the professional training—education, as you are talking about, that could be an incentive. But I wouldn't expect them to stay more than 5 years. Then you want to bring back the people who are out 10 years and bring them back at the proper level of the Government and not force them back into that civil service arrangement. Then you get the best of both worlds.

Mr. RICHMOND. Any ideas, Dr. Ralls.

Mr. RALLS. Yes, one is internship opportunities. I think as I mentioned, we have a unique internship with the U.S. Senate Sergeant at Arms scholarship for service, expanding that program. Right now, that program is limited to 4-year students. Community college students can get in through a backdoor through partnering with 4-year institutions, but expanding that, such as the 2017 Cyber Scholarship Act that is been suggested.

Another area that is not necessarily private or public, but cuts across both is the requirements for Federal contracting. So certain things can limit students who are coming out of colleges, whether 4-year or 2-year, particularly for 2-year students into roles because of those either experience requirements that kind-of put them in a double-edged sword that they may not have the years of experience that are required, and so—but they have to be able to get that experience, or also many of the Federal contracting requirements are very degree-based, require 4-year credentials and are not as skills-based. So that can limit students who may be coming out of a community college, looking at a foothold in a job role, and then going back and getting their bachelor's degree. So looking at contracting requirements is another area to pay attention to.

Mr. RICHMOND. Mr. Jarvis, very quickly, what are the challenges associated with setting aside the conventional wisdom that degrees equals skills and integrating these strategies into work force development plans?

Mr. JARVIS. Yes, no, that is an excellent question. I mean, I think there is a transition that needs to happen. I think that is what at IBM have been advocating for here in the past year is really trying to shine a light on the issue to look past degrees and to look at skills to help us with our most challenging and pressing information technology skills gaps, you know, not only in cybersecurity in particular.

I do think it is a bit of a culture change, and I do think it will take a little bit of time, but that is why we are trying to advocate for our clients and for others in the field that are—you know, that are suffering from the same gaps to expand the aperture and to look at new sources of talent.

Mr. RICHMOND. Very quickly, Dr. Ralls, what can we do to increase the number of minorities and women and African-Americans in the cyber space?

Mr. RALLS. Well, I think all of us—and that includes what we are doing at our community college—we have to be very aggressive in our approaches to pull students through. I mean, in areas like computer programming and cybersecurity, we do not see as many female students and you don't see as many female students in the work force. So that is where we have to work closely with our public schools. We have to change our marketing materials. We have to have different forms of outreach in that regard.

We also have to have role models in our programs so that we have to make sure that we are recruiting and aggressive about recruiting female and minority teachers. The leader of our cybersecurity program is female, and I do think that makes a difference, as well. So I think we each have to be aggressive in our own ways to make sure that students, regardless of gender or regardless of background, know that the opportunities are there, but also know that the ladder is there to be able to get there. That is why I think community colleges are so important in this role, to help provide a front end for that ladder to those opportunities, which many students may not think is possible for them.

Mr. RATCLIFFE. I thank the gentleman. Chair now recognizes the Chairman of the Subcommittee on Higher Education and Workforce Development, Mr. Guthrie.

Mr. GUTHRIE. Thanks. It is interesting what Mr. Jarvis just said. The Ranking Member, Ms. Davis, and I have been looking at programs that don't necessarily—education systems that allow people to have careers that don't necessarily require degrees if the skills needed don't require degrees. I think it would be very helpful, even not just for people in high schools moving forward, but also people trying to get relocated, understanding there is a skills gap. They are in—maybe even have a degree, but not in the right program, not in the degree to take advantage of the opportunities that are out there, and then being able to plug back in is something we really want to look at.

Mr. Rapp, I was just kind-of—as I was looking preparing for this hearing, my son did information technology, computer science and so forth. What are the skills—and there is a shortage there, too. As that, that worked out, because he was able to get a good job, but it is not good for the country, so we got to fill that in. So I guess the question is: What is the difference between somebody in information technology, the skills, and cybersecurity? I know they overlap, but what just kind of distinct differences?

Mr. RAPP. They do. You know, in conversations with the CSOs that represent our membership, the foundation for both tend to root itself in that analytical side and the coding side, awesome. The biggest skills that our members look forward, that our membership looks forward is the problem-solving and the critical thinking skills.

What our CSOs say is that they can teach somebody the environment that they are working in. Certainly a foundation in risk and risk mitigation, but what is mostly lacking as a skill set from the students that are being produced today is that critical thinking and problem-solving ability.

Mr. GUTHRIE. So you can teach someone to code. The question is, can you teach someone to figure out how somebody is going to undo their code or try to get into their code and think through that——

Mr. RAPP. That is correct.

Mr. GUTHRIE. Is that the way to put it? So, Dr. Cambone, last week, the Education Department urged schools and colleges to strengthen their cybersecurity measures in response to all-on attacks in which cyber criminals have sought to extort money from educational institutions on the threat of releasing sensitive data from student records. These records contain sensitive information and must be protected with stronger security.

What additional steps do you think institutions with cybersecurity programs can take to ensure they are developing a robust cybersecurity work force that can help prevent these types of intrusions?

Mr. CAMBONE. Well, first, we need to make sure that the—that which we teach we actually do.

Mr. GUTHRIE. Is that——

Mr. CAMBONE. Right? So it is not enough to teach these things. We have to do them. I am happy to say that I have had over the last 3 weeks a number of conversations with the university system-level CSOs, as well as the folks at the A&M level, and they are quite attentive to the need. So they are doing the things that you would expect them to do.

Mr. GUTHRIE. So what would be some of the examples of things that they are——

Mr. CAMBONE. Well, you know, we have moved past merely watching the firewalls, and we are now very attentive, for example, not just to the presence of odd e-mail in the system, but we are actually now capable of putting out the alerts very quickly on the phishing attacks that one gets—I just had one today, as a matter of fact, describing in detail precisely what that attack looks like, what you are supposed to do in response and the like. So there is a very active set of measures in place.

Mr. GUTHRIE. OK, thank you. Thank you for that. Mr. Jarvis, in your testimony and when you wrote and you discussed that the fact that the House has passed the Strengthening Career and Technical Education for the 21st Century Act, what we calmly call here the Perkins Act, the bill is now awaiting Senate action. If Perkins CTE is reauthorized, how do you think it will help employers more effectively address their cybersecurity work force needs?

Mr. JARVIS. Yes, certainly, certainly. Well, I mean, simply put, you know, education needs to produce the people that we need to hire. I think we believe that in passing CTE, you know, that is going to build the pipeline for us in the long term and it is going to support that pipeline in the long term for us, because we just can't look at it in terms of a—you know, it is just not a point problem, right? We need to do this for many, many years, and I think it is going to keep and expand the pool of applicants and the pool of experts that we need.

Mr. GUTHRIE. I think you are right. Been really looking at this with Ranking Member Davis and I in discussing a lot of it is, a generation ago, back when I was in high school, a generation ago, that was 30-something years ago, we really got away from technical and pushing training, and we are paying for it now. So we can't just take a short-term view, which we absolutely need. We also need to take a long-term view about what is good for the overall system, so a generation from now, we are not saying, well, we should have addressed, done more. So that is important.

Mr. JARVIS. Exactly.

Mr. GUTHRIE. Well, thank you very much. My time is about to expire, but I will yield back.

Mr. RATCLIFFE. Thank the gentleman. Chair now recognizes the Ranking Minority Member of the Subcommittee on Higher Education and Workforce Development, Ms. Davis, for 5 minutes.

Ms. DAVIS. Thank you. Thank you very much, Mr. Chairman. I want to relate to the comments of my colleague, Mr. Guthrie, because I think if we could open our minds and our hearts in many ways on this issue of how do you create better pathways for young people, not necessarily relying on a more traditional college track, and doing something I think in Switzerland they call it permeable, so that you have young people moving from certification to—into the colleges and back, and certification. I think there is a different route that is possible out there. That is also attributable to the issue that I think we are dealing with right now.

How do you create that better for young people so they aspire to those areas, but there is also a lot of prestige in their moving forward so that you get a lot more community acceptance? I think it all sort of fits together. Dr. Ralls, I wondered if you could speak a little bit to the NOVA program for a second, because I think you were able to do some work particularly in helping to transition veterans and students more seamlessly into the job market there. What—are there some surprises in trying to do that? How do you see being able to scale more of those efforts as you look at other programs connected so strongly to the community college system?

Mr. RALLS. Well, I will start first with high schools and working with the high schools. So one of the things that many people do not realize is one of the fastest-growing areas of community college enrollment is dual enrollment with high school students. Essentially—when Mr. Jarvis is talking about P–TECH, that is a dual enrollment strategy. So what we have to do a better job of is taking our pathways into programs into high schools.

So one of the challenges for us is that—as challenging as it is for us to employ cybersecurity professionals at the community-college level, you can imagine at the high-school level. So what we really have to do—and I think this is important around how we collaborate through Perkins funding and other things—is to make sure our pathways connect with each other so that students can start in high school and finish and move through community colleges and move on through universities. I think paying attention to that is very important.

We pay very, very close attention to our veterans' population, because we see that is such a rich resource for the cybersecurity work force in our region. We have over 7,000 veterans at our college, one of the largest populations of veterans in the United States. They bring with—well, you know, all the marvelous attributes.

We have then similarly with public schools, we are working to reach in to particularly our partners with the Marine Corps, working with military before they transition out, first making sure that they articulate, because they pick up technical skills along the way in terms of military occupational specialties, being very aggressive about that, being very nimble about how we provide education to them over very concentrated short periods of time, what we call surge programs, and then making sure that the education they are receiving in the military transitions through us, as well.

So again, this is much about not just waiting for students to come to us, but to reach into those valuable pools to make sure students are starting along a valuable pathway as they move forward.

Ms. DAVIS. Yes, thank you. I appreciate that, because in some ways, I think what you are suggesting is there may be opportunities that maybe for someone who has been trained in a number of the industries within the military to shorten their training period when it comes to cybersecurity. You are talking about months, not years, and maybe there are other programs that have done something similar.

If I may just, Mr. Jarvis, going to you quickly, because I know that one of the needs you have in finding trained personnel is sometimes going to other countries where you have an easier time doing that. Is it fair to say that if we don't answer the need with our own students that a number of companies will continue to do, as you have to do today, to look elsewhere?

Mr. JARVIS. I am not really expert on that particular area for IBM, but, I mean, you know, we are going to look for the talent where we need to find the talent. We want to develop it wherever we can. We have a global business, so we are obviously looking all across the globe for that talent, wherever it may be.

Ms. DAVIS. Yes. Well, we want to make sure that companies like IBM find those resources in our own country. Yes. One or two—well, I think my time is up, Mr. Chairman, so perhaps I know I am going to hear everybody else asking the same questions. Thank you very much.

Mr. RATCLIFFE. Thank the gentlelady. The Chair now recognizes the Chairwoman of the full committee of Education and Workforce, the gentlelady from North Carolina, Ms. Foxx.

Ms. FOXX. Thank you very much. I do have some questions, but I have to first make a comment about Mr. Rapp's talking about the fact that we need people who have problem-solving and critical thinking skills and say to all of my colleagues and all of the panelists, if we continue to use that train word, which I hate so much, you are not going to encourage critical thinking. So I want to ask you all, Dr. Ralls, to take it out of your vocabulary and all of us.

Honestly, there is no better example of what I am talking about than his just saying that. You remember, you train animals and you educate people. So if you want critical thinking, you have got to be in the education business.

Mr. Rapp, I will come back to you. Indiana included the SkillUp! grant program in the combined State work force development plan the State developed to implement the changes passed as part of

WIOA. In your experience, how has the SkillUp! program been integrated with Indiana's broader work force development efforts?

Mr. RAPP. Indiana has done an outstanding job, working particularly with the Department of Workforce Development under the last commissioner, Steve Braun, who spent a lot of time taking data and ensuring that the data was correct so it accurately reflected what the needs were of the State.

In accordance with what he found through that, the SkillUp! program now is driven by the demand of the employers as that data was collected directly from the employers. So that goes to my point earlier that—in public-private partnerships, we have to get as close to the source of data as possible to make it accurate, and then we must tailor with the resources that we have currently—we must tailor those limited resources to the demand so that we can have the best effectiveness of those programs.

Ms. FOXX. So would you say a little bit more about how you are measuring the success?

Mr. RAPP. Right now, the success that we measure is literally by both the unemployment rate specifically for cybersecurity. We do rely heavily on a public-private partnership from NICE, CompTIA, and Fireglass, I believe, the Cyberseek program. What that program does is it surveys all the States for the job listings and then the number of jobs that are filled. So that is fairly accurate data, so that is how we are able to measure that, particularly within that area.

I will say with 32 universities in Indiana that offer cybersecurity curriculum with seven different centers of excellence, DHS, NSA, and six R1 through R3 research institutions, we are very proud of all of those things. But we are still not yet gaining ground.

Ms. FOXX. Mr. Jarvis, I am a strong advocate for earn and learn programs that provide students and job seekers the opportunity to learn on the job. Nobody knows better than employers what skills are needed to succeed in a particular career. So what suggestions do you have to better align our academic programs with potential on-the-job learning opportunities?

Mr. JARVIS. Certainly, certainly. I think that one of the things that we look for in terms of learning—we were talking about critical thinking a little bit earlier—is we look across the board, and especially in cybersecurity, to make sure that our candidates are explorers, they are consultants, they are students, they are guardians, and they are also problem solvers. I think those are all things that that can come through earn and learn.

Whether it is through the P–TECH model, where we have students basically guaranteed internships as part of their education program, so they are both learning and earning and learning some more as part of the process, or if it is through internships or apprenticeships or other programs that we have, and we think those are all important and are part of the solution.

Ms. FOXX. Well, thank you all very much. In my clips today—I haven't had a chance to read it—there is an article that says United States needs to move past its fixation on the bachelor's degree, studies say. It is in *Education Week* by Catherine Gewertz. I am going to get a copy of it and see, because I know this is an issue that is come up several times here this morning.

Thank you all very much. I yield back, Mr. Chairman.

Mr. RATCLIFFE. Thank the Chairwoman. Chair now recognizes the Ranking Member of the full committee on Education and Workforce, Mr. Scott, the gentleman from Virginia.

Mr. SCOTT. Thank you, Mr. Chairman. I thank the witnesses for being with us today.

Mr. Cambone, you went to great lengths to say how you fashion your curriculum to address the needs of the industry. Is there value in making sure that what is in your curriculum in Texas is the same that is in the curriculum in Virginia, so that people who present with a cybersecurity degree will be presenting the same credentials?

Mr. CAMBONE. Hmm, it is an interesting question. My instincts say yes. But my respect for the academic integrity of the various institutions leads me to think and to expect that there will be some differences. That is not bad. So what we have—one of our members is very active in a National curriculum consortium. What they do is share both best practices and where the leading edge of education is going to answer, in part, what you are suggesting, which is there needs to be some conforming of the knowledge that is being imparted.

Mr. SCOTT. Well, who would put together the standard?

Mr. CAMBONE. You know, I think that is best left to the educators. I think that, as I say——

Mr. SCOTT. A consortium, as you have suggested, so that you would have some kind of independent judge?

Mr. CAMBONE. I think that would be very helpful. If we did the cyber grant arrangement, that would be a mechanism for doing that kind of conforming.

Mr. SCOTT. Thank you. Mr. Jarvis, last year, the EEOC issued a report on diversity in the tech industry. The findings were that racial discrimination and ethnic discrimination was wide-spread in the tech industry, such that if they stopped discriminating, there would not be a shortage of workers in the tech industry. Is the cybersecurity part of the tech industry plagued with that problem?

Mr. JARVIS. I don't know specifically in terms of—I mean, I couldn't speak to specifics in terms of the problem. I mean, I do think we need to do a lot more outreach. I do think we need to do a lot more recruitment. I do think that IBM does a fairly good job at reaching out to underserved groups traditionally and reaching for that. I think for cybersecurity, it is just as important, talking about some of the professional organizations that are out there that we recruit at. I think that is one thing that can be done, but I think there is other things, as well.

Mr. SCOTT. I understand that there is a net downsizing at IBM, yet you still import thousands of H–1B guest workers. Can you explain the apparent discrepancy?

Mr. JARVIS. That is not really my area of expertise, but we could probably get more information for you if you need it.

Mr. SCOTT. OK, that would be good. Dr. Ralls, can you tell us what barriers there are to apprenticeship and internships in the cybersecurity area?

Mr. RALLS. Well, to have internship and apprenticeships, you have to have a strong commitment from the employer community.

Many employers do step up. That is one of the great things for us is our partnership with Year Up, which has managed I think across the country, is doing a remarkable job in cultivating internships for deserving young people that are moving into IT and cyber and finance areas. So that is been a great partnership for us, working with companies like Amazon, now that is sponsoring its first apprenticeship.

Apprenticeship is new to IT. So I think it is evolving in that regard. It does take a great deal of employer commitment. One of the things with our apprenticeship programs, for instance, if you look at our apprenticeship with Amazon Web Services, which is focused around cloud security, that is primarily based around certifications. It is a 16-week program where we provide the related training, so it is security plus, Linux plus, plus they get the AWS architect certification.

One of the things that Congress can do is look at the opening up the notion of what certifications mean in the workplace as a workplace credential, areas like Pell Grants for short-term certifications that are meaningful and have rigor—I think can open up more opportunities for apprenticeship opportunities and for those kinds of certification programs that we find are important with apprenticeship.

Mr. SCOTT. Are you able to leverage the WIOA and CTE funds for those programs?

Mr. RALLS. We are, for those students who are eligible, so with, for instance, our AWS apprenticeship program, some of those students are able to be supported through WIOA, because they qualify. A few are also supported through a group called Apprenti, which is I think supported through apprenticeship funding. Then we also support some ourselves. So looking at how those opportunities are available, certainly they are all employees of the company and they will move into new career ladders or new job payment ladders as a result of their involvement in apprenticeships.

So I do think apprenticeship is something that there are many ways to open up the doors much more than we have those opportunities. IT and cyber I think are rich for that because of the connections with particularly certification opportunities that can tie into some of these program areas.

Mr. RATCLIFFE. I thank the gentleman. Chair now recognizes the gentleman from Pennsylvania, Mr. Thompson, for 5 minutes.

Mr. THOMPSON. Chairman, thank you. Gentlemen and panel, thank you for bringing your experience and expertise. I want to start with Mr. Rapp. You know, I am proud of two institutions of learning I have. I have a number of them in the district, but in terms of cybersecurity, you know, Penn State and also in the northwestern part of the district, Mercyhurst, we have got the Tom Ridge School of Cybersecurity there in Erie County.

Mr. Rapp, the degrees required for many cybersecurity programs are only 2 years in length. What advantage does a 2-year cybersecurity credential offer over a 4-year-plus program? Plus, any thoughts on—for lack of a better word—micro-degrees, less than 2-year type certification programs?

Mr. RAPP. Well, that is a great question. What we found is there is different skills that are required for different functionalities in cybersecurity. Not every single person in cybersecurity needs to have a 4-year degree. That is true. So the rise of applied 2-year cybersecurity degrees have been directed toward a gap of applied entry-level cybersecurity jobs that are out there.

Certifications are useful for, again, specific types of jobs. So I think there is a need across the spectrum for all of these degrees, and none of them should be discounted. I also believe that even beyond these degrees and certification, you know, when we look at what NICE has done to describe what skills are necessary to take part in work force development in cybersecurity, that we shouldn't discount aptitude testing outside of degrees.

Mr. THOMPSON. Well, thank you. Mr. Cambone, I understand Texas A&M believes work force development to be a core component of the institution mission. How does this affect the education experience you provide to your students?

Mr. CAMBONE. Well, sir, a very large fraction—and maybe my colleagues behind me can remind me—but a very large fraction of our incoming freshmen are first-time university students. So the focus is on retention of those students, bringing them all the way through to their graduation, because it is not helpful to start and not finish.

So you begin there. Then we have talked about the apprenticeship programs. We have talked about the internships. We have talked about the hack for defense programs. All of those kinds of things are intimately connected with their development. In the engineering school, they have to at the end participate in what amounts to a capstone project, where a number of them have to get together and figure out how to produce an outcome.

So all of that is part of the development of the student as a productive member of society and a member of the work force. With respect to the cyber business in particular, there are any number of—and I can give you a list of the extracurriculars that are in place—that the students, while they are not required to engage, find themselves wanting to engage because it doesn't bring them an experience that they are not going to get just in the classroom. So it gives them the opportunity to apply what they have learned as they go forward.

So all of that, you roll all that up and you do some of the placement work that is necessary, then for those students to find jobs when they are finished, and that is how you take someone who is first-time university and their families to a position in the work force.

Mr. THOMPSON. Thank you. Dr. Ralls, from your written testimony, I saw cybersecurity job posting growth 74 percent since 2014. That is amazing. At the Northern Virginia area, two times as likely given job opportunities here for positions, position opportunities. Is your program currently at capacity for enrollment? What specific strategies do you use for recruitment?

Mr. RALLS. Well, we are not at capacity, but we do struggle primarily to make sure that we can acquire the instructors that we need. We are moving down multiple strategies in terms of facilities. We also have to make sure that we can look for strategies to pay our instructors higher rates so that we can keep them.

One of the things—having the highest concentration of cyberse-curity jobs in the country, which also means we have the highest concentration of valuable adjunct faculty in our region, and so we tap into that very aggressively. But we also share. We work very closely with all our partners around the country. I think that is the value of, for instance, like the NSA–CAE programs. Austin Community College was with us yesterday. We worked with the other 22 community colleges in our State, in terms of acquiring that CAE designation, and we also provide much of the instruction on-line—we operate the shared services backbone for the on-line instruction in our State, so many students are—at other parts of our State, in rural southwest Virginia, and taking cybersecurity programs through their institutions, but acquiring some of the classwork through us on-line because we have the valuable instructional re-source in our region. We just have to look for strategies to get those resources out broadly into areas where they may not actually natu-rally exist.

Mr. RATCLIFFE. I thank the gentleman. The Chair now recognizes the gentleman from Connecticut, Mr. Courtney, for 5 minutes.

Mr. COURTNEY. Thank you, Mr. Chairman, and thank both sub-committees for holding this hearing and to all the witnesses that are here. You know, listening to the sort-of to-do list in terms of where Congress can help, I was struck by the fact that as someone who sits on the Armed Services Committee, the last defense au-thorization bill that was just signed in December by President Obama actually raised the Cyber Command to parity with the full other combatant commands, which is saying something, you know, in terms of the fact that, you know, we have got to sort-of be more agile in terms of how we think about this issue and address it.

Again, the nice thing about this hearing is, again, we are talking about pathways other than just 4-year degrees. Dr. Ralls, you talked about the Amazon apprenticeship program. I mean, Amazon is almost as big as the Pentagon it seems like these days. So, I mean, they obviously have a lot more capability in terms of taking on an apprenticeship program with a work force of tens of thou-sands of people. The challenge that I am hearing out there for a lot of smaller firms who are—whether it is a small community bank that is, you know, terrified about cyber attacks or small de-fense suppliers that are as much a back door to cyber attacks as the large OEMs.

It is just that, you know, they don't think in terms of their human resources or apprenticeship sort-of models. How we can sort-of get them engaged, I guess, is—you know, the question I was going to ask. I mean, it sounds like a really impressive program that you have with Amazon, but, I mean, have you been able to sort-of break through to smaller employers in terms of getting them engaged in apprenticeships?

Mr. RALLS. Well, first, I think it is important to keep in mind, you know, the Amazon program is a cloud security program. In fact, you have to thread a pretty good needle to get into, for in-stance, the veterans program. You already have to have a bach-elor's degree, a network plus certification, and be a veteran. So it is—you know, you are going to a certain place.

But one thing that I think that is important to keep in mind with cybersecurity is, it is broad. Cybersecurity is broad. So I think all institutions are having to take a cyber mentality. So even though students coming out may not—for instance, we graduate more information technology associate's degree graduates of any community college in the country. IT graduates, networking students who are going in have a cyber mentality, and that is also a foothold for them to move up and actually gain the credentials to be technically cybersecurity.

I think there are other places, too, that community colleges, if I may, are naturally inclined to help. A lot of times we think about attacks that are only coming through computers, but we are—there are more network devices now than there are people in the world. So technicians, facility maintenance have to take on new mentalities around cybersecurity.

There is an OT side to cybersecurity. So, for instance, we are working on programs, programs that when I was in North Carolina we developed and here we are working—we have, for instance, the largest data center work force and employment in the country. Well, a technician today has to be able to know, is something a maintenance failure? Or is your HVAC system being hacked? Is your PLC being hacked? So I think cyber is really much broader than the narrow term of specific IT cybersecurity programs. We have to make sure we make the linkages in terms of that breadth.

Mr. COURTNEY. I guess my point—in terms of trying to get employers to think about apprenticeships, just as a model——

Mr. RALLS. Apprenticeship.

Mr. COURTNEY. Yes, just, you know—I mean, so to bring it back to Congress, there is a Department of Labor apprenticeship grant program which President Trump's budget actually called for funding at last year's level. It was eliminated in the House appropriations bill. The Senate actually fully funded it. So those funds in Connecticut, I can just tell you, have been a really good enticement to get companies that never really sort-of thought about getting involved in apprenticeships to actually do it, you know, to make that job and to doing it.

I guess that is the question is: How do we entice small guys to get into the business of apprenticeships?

Mr. RALLS. Yes, apprenticeship is not easy. Apprenticeship takes a great commitment. I worked with Siemens and Bosch—and I know how much investment they put in per student. So IT is moving more that direction, I think primarily because of the gaps they see. I think IT is naturally inclined that way, but I do think we do have to do more than just talk about apprenticeship. We have to have meaningful programs for apprenticeship. I think we also have to look broadly at being very aggressive around just meaningful work-based learning.

Sometimes we have programs that aren't formal apprenticeship, but they are very much important because of that work-based learning. Because for many students coming out of our colleges and universities now, many of them, unlike when I was a student, they didn't work in high school. They didn't have some of those opportunities. So apprenticeship becomes even more important, I believe, for today's students, apprenticeship and meaningful work-based learning than it is ever had before. So I do think that is a very important area for us to collectively pay attention to.

Mr. COURTNEY. Thank you, Mr. Chairman.

Mr. RATCLIFFE. Thank the gentleman. The Chair now recognizes the gentleman from Pennsylvania, Mr. Smucker, for 5 minutes.

Mr. SMUCKER. Thank you, Mr. Chairman. Dr. Ralls, two things you mentioned in your testimony I would like to follow up on. You had mentioned Year Up, and I would be interested in understanding—I wonder if you could elaborate a little more on the partnership that you have with Year Up. Do Year Up recruits attend class at your school? Or are they recruited from the school? If you would just elaborate on that, I would appreciate it.

Mr. RALLS. Yes, Year Up is a National work force development organization. Started in the Northeast. A model has emerged—our college has been a lead in working with Europe because of such a complementary relationship. Essentially what Year Up does is it provides a 1-year experience for students, and it is where they gain professional workplace skills through supplemental instruction. They have meaningful internships. They receive financial support. What we provide is the technical instruction through our education programs through the community college.

Perhaps maybe I could give you an example, though, because I will tell you of a student example which I think explains why it is such a natural fit with community colleges. One of our students is a great student named Darwin who last year was served on our community college board as the student representative. Darwin grew up in foster youth homes, four foster youth homes. He came to our college in high school through our outreach programs in the high school, found about Year Up, and became involved in the Year Up program.

So his experience last semester, he was describing it to me recently, he worked 5 days a week in an internship with Freddie Mac. He would take special supplemental classes that help him in terms of making sure he has the critical thinking, the workplace skills that add to the value. He took two cyber classes with us at night at our Reston Center, and then he took two classes on-line.

Then on Saturdays, he would go to our Woodbridge campus and work in a program that we have called—not work, we have many students that come and meet with our instructors on Saturdays to do competitions and other types of things called CyberAll. So Darwin is an example of the kind of individual that without the doors that can reach out through programs like our community colleges, like Year Up, it is an example of how you can go from the bottom 20 percent to the top 20 percent, as long as you have got that ladder and that work opportunity to get there, and Year Up is key to us as a complementary partner in that regard.

Mr. SMUCKER. Yes, it sounds like a great program. I would like to follow up, as well, on the discussion on apprenticeships. I will go to Dr. Cambone and potentially come back to you, Dr. Ralls, if we have time. But I am very interested in apprenticeship programs, as well. One of the models that I have seen is a partnership with a college, a community college or another institution where there is an ability for an apprenticeship to both work on a job site and get a degree, whether it is an associate degree, or even a bachelor's.

I guess that is my question to you. Are you doing that? Is there a possibility of apprentices earning a bachelor's degree at the same time that they would earn a certificate, some sort of work certificate, as well?

Mr. CAMBONE. I am not precisely sure of whether that particular thing can be done. But this is what I do know. I mentioned earlier that A&M has a very close relationship with Blinn College. Blinn College is a very large, 2-year institution in the next city. We have a relationship with them that does take their students through apprenticeship programs, through the accreditation on the 2-year school matriculating to A&M and get your degree. So there is a ladder, as was described here, that can allow students to do that.

Not all students want to do it, right? So they are happy to take the off-ramps and pursue their lives in the way that they would like. But that ladder has been built.

Mr. SMUCKER. Yes, Dr. Ralls, would you like to respond to that, as well?

Mr. RALLS. I think the important thing for apprenticeship is that we have to make sure we structure it into our programs. So when students go through related training, that means that we have to make sure, for instance, if we are offering certifications through a related training, that we also structure so that we can give that credit as it comes through.

So I think more and more what we collectively have to do as educators is not look for the either/ors, but to make sure that those types of experiences, apprenticeship, particularly if it leads to certification and how we can give credit, military in terms of military occupational specialty, I think there are—you know, I think we get used to the either/ors.

Many of the students who come to us as a community college already have 4-year degrees. So they are looking to get specific skill sets on top of their 4-year degrees that allow them to enter into the workplace. So one of the things that is incumbent on educators is to make sure that we can structure our programs such that students can gain skills through things like apprenticeship, but make sure that they stack, if you will, or become a part of a program so that they can keep moving forward. I think that is very important in how we think about our educational curriculum structures.

Mr. SMUCKER. Very much agree. Thank you.

Mr. RATCLIFFE. I thank the gentleman. The Chair now recognizes the gentlelady from North Carolina, Ms. Adams, for 5 minutes.

Ms. ADAMS. Thank you, Mr. Chairman. I want to thank the Chairs and the Ranking Members of both subcommittees for coming together to convene this hearing today. Thank you for your testimony, gentlemen.

Dr. Ralls, in your testimony, you mentioned the great work of NOVA to fill the shortage of talent in the cybersecurity work force. You mentioned efforts to reach into underserved and untapped populations, speaking specifically of your campaign to encourage women, to explore careers. So have you explored ways to accomplish the same success with minority candidates?

Mr. RALLS. Well, I may sound like I am repeating myself, but I do think Year Up is a key factor for us in that regard. So if you look at the Year Up student population, it is primarily minority. So students from—as we refer to as opportunity youth through Year Up, and so I think that is a key strategy for us, because it is particularly focused on IT careers, also finance careers, and so that is an example.

For us, NOVA is a majority-minority institution. Diversity is kind-of in our core, it is in our being. So the chances are for most of our students, they are going to be from minority backgrounds. Where we have struggled is not having—is not so much around minority students coming through our programs, but in terms of female students. So that is why we have this year very deliberate outreach strategies with respect to female students.

But certainly I think our Year Up partnership is a key in terms of our reaching more minority students both male and female. For us at NOVA, that is a natural for us in terms of who we are.

Ms. ADAMS. OK, you say that NOVA has nine university partners where students can complete their degrees. Do you have any figures on how many of your graduates have transitioned to minority-serving institutions?

Mr. RALLS. I would have to get those to you in terms of HBCUs. I can't tell you specifically right now. I do know we are working right now on a partnership among universities and community colleges, actually with our veterans population, and one of the partners is Norfolk State, who has been a close partner in terms of working with one of our largest partners, which is George Mason University. So there is a collaborative of which Norfolk State is involved in that regard. So we certainly have had many students that have gone to HBCU programs. There are some cyber programs out there, as well, that would allow them to move forward with HBCUs.

Ms. ADAMS. Thank you. One of the ways to, I think, fix the lack of diversity in this industry is to encourage women and minorities to become entrepreneurs. Does NOVA have any special programs that encourage entrepreneurship?

Mr. RALLS. Yes, we do. In fact, at our Alexandria campus, we have a very unique program that is really—I have to give credit to our students and some really unique faculty there. They call themselves the Start Up Club. They actually—they are technology tinkerers. They meet with faculty in a small, little—I think it was probably a closet at one time, but they have multiple different tools there that they use. Last year, we sent them off to Cornell, and they came home with a second place cybersecurity competition award.

So we don't have as many resources around entrepreneurship, so we are partnering very closely right now with George Mason University around all aspects of tight connections. One of the areas that we are working and talking with them about is how we tap into their entrepreneurship programs.

One of the things that we don't always have to do is recreate the wheel when we can look for valuable partners. I do think our—and our university partners provide us a lot of opportunity to partner, to bring opportunities to community college students that they typically don't naturally have that you would find in terms of entrepreneurship programs that you see at universities.

Ms. ADAMS. Thank you. Quickly, Mr. Jarvis, do you have any figures on how successful your efforts have been in retaining female talent and how many women cybersecurity professionals at IBM remain after 3 years on the job?

Mr. JARVIS. Sure. I don't have the demographics in front of me at the moment. But, I mean, what I can do say is, you know, we do push very hard. In fact, the last three chief information security officers at IBM have been women. I think what is important is they provide being role models and mentors. We also have a very strong support network or professional organization within the company called Women and Security Excelling. That is a professional development and support organization for women in our cybersecurity group, providing role models, and they do host those cyber day for girls programs, as well.

So I think being able to have those professional support mechanisms, once we get the talent, helps us retain the talent.

Ms. ADAMS. Thank you very much. I am out of time. Mr. Chair, I yield back.

Mr. RATCLIFFE. Thank the gentlelady. Chair now recognizes my friend, the gentleman from Georgia, Mr. Allen.

Mr. ALLEN. Thank you, Mr. Chairman. It is great to be with you today. I am very interested in this education process. In fact, in my 12th Congressional District of Georgia, we have—are moving the U.S. Army Cyber Command. It is moving to Fort Gordon, and it has been a big—a lot of noise as far as my home town in the district, which is going to create about 12,000 cyber jobs in that district.

Our area has come together to embrace this opportunity. Public-private solutions have been critical to the success of the Army Cyber Command's relocation, and I am proud of my community coming together to forge a path for success. I would highlight two examples. Augusta University created a cyber institute to educate a local cyber work force, and our Governor Deal has just committed $50 million for a Georgia cyber innovation and training center dedicated to public-private partnerships and a cyber work force.

We also have the technical tinkerers club, and I have a robot on my desk that some elementary school children coded and built, and they didn't even know they did it. If you would have asked them to code them, they probably would have said—or if you were to ask a middle-schooler or a high-schooler, you know, we need you to code this, they would say, well, I can't do that. But these young people really embrace this.

To the extent that what I found in serving on the Education and Workforce Committee, one is there is a huge disconnect between the business community and the education community. Second is that, for example, in Dublin, Georgia, we have an inner city school system that went to two charter elementary schools. One is on leadership. It is teaching Stephen Covey's seven habits. The other one is a STEM school. We now have a 96 percent graduation rate in an inner city school system. This career direction idea is extremely important.

We also note, if you are not reading at a third-grade level when you get to the fourth grade, you are likely you are not going to graduate. For some reason, when they get to middle school, we lose them. I mean, middle school the teachers say is just a real issue here with keeping focus on education.

So with those challenges, you know, we are talking about college, we are talking about high school. I am not sure we don't need to go back to the elementary school and really try to help these young people understand exactly why they are getting an education. Because I asked them what their dreams are every time I go. They have great dreams. They just don't know what they are doing there.

So I would just like to go down the entire panel there and just get your ideas on—do we need to kind-of get thinking out of the box here and figure out what in the heck is wrong? Because the United States is not where we need to be as far as education. We are losing a lot of young people. They are not focused. They don't know where they want to go.

So, Mr. Cambone.

Mr. CAMBONE. Yes, sir. Well, I am happy to say that I was just in Augusta not 10 days ago——

Mr. ALLEN. It is exciting, isn't it?

Mr. CAMBONE [continuing]. Talking with Dr. Sexton. She has got a terrific crew of people there. We are hoping we are going to partner with them moving forward. So I wanted to let you know that.

Second, on the education, I couldn't agree with you more. My wife is a grade school teacher of now nigh on to 40 years. She would give you one answer: Read. They have to be read to at home.

Mr. ALLEN. Yes, we have mentors, a program now, mentor program where we have mentors go into the schools and read what these kids are interested in. It is amazing, a light bulb just goes off. Mr. Rapp.

Mr. RAPP. I would like to say, too, then that I am a graduate of Fort Gordon. I spent 34 years in the Army, the last 3 in Army Cyber, and our CPT right now is on mission.

Mr. ALLEN. Thank you for your service.

Mr. RAPP. Absolutely. I would have to agree with reading. I think the other thing is teaching good cyber hygiene habits early, so teaching children safety and how to utilize technology.

Mr. ALLEN. Mr. Jarvis.

Mr. JARVIS. Yes, I definitely think—mentors that can provide some positive relatable examples I think are extremely important. Instilling digital literacy at an early age I think is just going to help in the long run. Just as kind-of an aside for the mentorship program, in one of the P–TECH schools that we sponsor in Baltimore, right, there are so many interested IBM'ers in helping mentor these kids that a lot of them have two mentors, which is great, I mean, because they can ask them questions and things like that, so I think that is essential.

Mr. ALLEN. That is important for the business community. I am out of time. Mr. Ralls, you can comment on that on the next question. But I will tell you that there are two college dropouts that made a big difference in this world, Bill Gates and Steve Jobs. So with that, thank you for being here today.

Mr. RATCLIFFE. Thank the gentleman. Chair now recognizes the gentleman from California, Mr. Takano, for 5 minutes.

Mr. TAKANO. Thank you, Mr. Chairman. I am glad to be here this afternoon to engage in this timely discussion on how to address the growing need for a strong and diverse cybersecurity work force. As the Vice Ranking Member of the House Veterans Affairs Committee and as a Member of its subcommittee on the economic opportunity, I understand the importance of providing the resources needed to allow our talented and skilled veterans to pursue cybersecurity opportunities after their service.

My first question is for Mr. Ralls. Mr. Ralls, you pointed to NOVA's efforts to support veterans in pursuit of a cybersecurity career. In particular, you mentioned a partnership with the United States Marines and Marine Corps University to provide surge educational opportunities. Can you share a bit more about the partnership surge educational opportunities?

Mr. RALLS. Yes, sir. What surge refers to is essentially our—collectively with the Marine Corps University and the Marine Corps—is to be nimble in how we provide concentrated instruction at times when military members are available and can be scheduled to receive that. So, for instance, short-week classes—or multi-week classes that are shorter than an average semester or even mini-semester. Same number of hours, but in a very concentrated way, so being able to do that.

Then also being able to, first, recognize military occupational specialties, so there is about 10 MOSs within the Marines that will lead between to 3 to 23 credit hours in terms of credit that can be received, depending on what that previous technical background is, making our programs flexible through distance education and other opportunities, as I mentioned, and then making sure they ladder so that Marines can complete our programs.

That is one of the reasons our State government and general assembly worked with us to—or led efforts to reduce tuition, so when Marines leave—may be deployed or go to other places, they don't have to pay out-of-State tuition.

A couple other things, too. One thing that we are working toward, boot camps—and I know boot camps have been mentioned—programming skills are key to cyber. We created a special boot camp just for veterans. It is a different model. We are still struggling and working our way through it, but to make it free of charge to veterans, that is a concentrated, almost 50- to 60-hour-week boot camp. So we are looking at different models because military members when they are in, they have periods of time for education. We have got to make that work. When they are out, they need to get into employment very quickly and to certain roles.

Mr. TAKANO. I note that you have active-duty service members in your program. Does tuition assistance from the Department of Defense help pay for their education?

Mr. RALLS. Absolutely, absolutely. Partly we want to make sure, too, when students leave and they may be classified as out-of-State, that was an effort to——

Mr. TAKANO. Has there been thought about how you coordinate the—well, counsel these service members on using their tuition assistance in combination with their G.I. Bill, how they can strategize to use that to their best benefit? My thought is that many service members, if they—once they leave the service, if they have already acquired a great deal of expertise and credit hours, they can try to bank their G.I. Bill and use it for a graduate degree. I mean, that kind of thinking, that kind of strategizing.

Do you—how do you identify your—the Marines, for example, that can go to your program? Do you self-identify? Do you market to——

Mr. RALLS. You are talking about in terms of active-duty Marines?

Mr. TAKANO. Yes.

Mr. RALLS. Primarily through our relationships with Quantico. So, you know, the relationship—on base, we have people stationed in base, but we also have such a strong relationship with Marine Corps University and others that this partnered—so those Marines who are there are aware of our programs. We are working to scale those programs with Marine Corps University beyond just cyber and other opportunities, as well.

Mr. TAKANO. This is really interesting to me, because we have a huge problem with the TAPS program being considered inadequate. As a teacher, former teacher, I have always thought that to be really, really—I don't know, not accurate, but to be true to the G.I. Bill, the promise of the G.I. Bill, what we use to pull people into the service, that we should assess the students on Day 1, set educational goals for them while they are in the service, encourage them to use tuition assistance to bring their skills up or, in this case, they are actually acquiring a major set of skills. Then the separation wouldn't be so traumatic or aimless or people—there is a much more seamless transition to civilian life.

Mr. RALLS. Yes. I would say, too, the partnership with—I have to give a lot of credit to our Marine partners. The Marines are very focused now, the commandant and others, in terms of the—making sure that all Marines have a credential, have a degree. So I think community colleges and these partnerships are key in that regard.

Mr. TAKANO. So my time is up. I want to explore—I hope we can get your information. I want to have our committee on the veterans side explore more about what you are doing. Thanks. I yield back, sir.

Mr. RATCLIFFE. Thank the gentleman. The Chair now recognizes the gentlelady from Delaware, Ms. Blunt Rochester, for 5 minutes.

Ms. BLUNT ROCHESTER. Thank you, Mr. Chairman. I want to thank the panel. Mr. Rapp, when you first talked about your son, that was really an interesting moment for me, because I sat here thinking about the fact that the battery on my phone is about to die, and I feel so vulnerable. I thought about the vulnerability of us as individuals with autonomous vehicles, internet of things, machine learning, artificial intelligence, blockchain, cloud computing, biotech.

I started running through all of these things that I had not thought about years back that are now before us. As a Nation, as businesspeople, as individuals, this conversation is vital. I have two perspectives to bring. One, I served as a State personnel director in the State of Delaware, and we had a shortage of IT professionals. One of the things that we had to look at is, what attracts them to the job and, also, how to retain them.

So one of my questions is really about, is there any research to suggest what would attract people to the field? That is the first question. Then the second is really around—because I met at NSA a young guy who came from a great school, and it wasn't the things that I would think would attract somebody to the job. It was something as simple as parking. Like, there were things that, you know, NSA needs parking.

But I am just curious, is there any research on what attracts people to the job? Also, the marketing aspect. Is there any marketing that is happening? Because some of these fields are things we never even heard about before, so a parent is not saying go be a cyber technician. They are saying go be an engineer or a doctor or a lawyer. Anybody, any advice on those?

Mr. RAPP. You know, I think, first of all, we have to break down some barriers. When we look at the romanticized version of working in the Valley, it seems very attractive until you get out there and you are sharing an 1,100-square-foot apartment with four other people.

But, you know, we also have to embrace change. As governments look toward attracting that type of talent, you know, there is some hard work that has to be done. You know, simple things like the scholarship for service, expanding that to State and local governments, you know, because we are as vulnerable from those aspects as we are from the Federal Government, because we all work together and our systems all interact. So we have got to get out of these verticals that we put ourselves in.

The other thing is, is we have to look at—you know, great example of a soldier who was trained by the United States Army, went to the CPT in Indiana, left the State of Indiana to go do this training, came back with more certifications than I can possibly remember, and then went back to the Government, and they told him that they couldn't hire him back in because he had come in at a much higher level and there was a rule that he couldn't make more money coming back in—that much more money coming back in.

We look at GS levels and things like that and the qualifications for jobs, those things were written decades ago and they need to be updated. So if you want to attract people to it, you have to speak a common language and a more modern language. Those are just a few observations there.

Security clearances, you know, higher education produces a lot of degrees, and it is—you know, it is lucrative to attract out-of-State, out-of-country tuition. So we are training people and sending them back to our competition. You know, and we in CLA like to work with the community colleges because they are more likely to have U.S. citizens. So when they go to find—go to get security clearances, if they can get one in a year or 18 months, then they have a better chance at doing that. Much of the work that is done in cybersecurity in the State of Indiana is defense-oriented.

Ms. BLUNT ROCHESTER. I have, like, less than a minute left. It is not your fault, mine. But, Dr. Cambone and Dr. Ralls, maybe afterwards, I was just curious about your relationships with the work force development systems. To me, I was around for WIA and

WIOA, and I am just curious if the relationships have been good, strong, better, worse?

Mr. RALLS. Our apprenticeship opportunity started with our work force board. Our chair of our college is also chair of our regional work force board, so we have a very unique synergy.

Ms. BLUNT ROCHESTER. Excellent.

Mr. CAMBONE. Yes, ma'am. It is very strong. We have got two agencies, actually, who spend a lot of time doing work force development across the entire spectrum. So the answer is yes.

Ms. BLUNT ROCHESTER. Got you. Then my last quick question, which we don't have time for, but I was just curious if background checks and security clearances limit the folks that are entering the field, and if that is a challenge, particularly with a lot of things that people are into these days, like marijuana?

Mr. CAMBONE. If I may, Mr. Chairman—yes.

[Laughter.]

Mr. CAMBONE. I had some experience with this back in my earlier career. The answer is two-fold. In certain respects, it has gotten less—your life is less a prohibition to your being granted a clearance, provided that you are straightforward in your testimony, if you will, in the forms that you fill out. If you live abroad, it is a little more complicated. But that has gotten a little easier.

The difficulty is we have a massive backlog. Getting the clearance is oftentimes the barrier to being able to do certain kinds of work. So we really do need to go back and rethink why we classify things the way we do and then how do we put the clearance process in place to match the kind of work that needs to be done. So not everything is Top Secret. So not everybody needs a Top-Secret clearance.

Ms. BLUNT ROCHESTER. Thank you.

Mr. CAMBONE. So can we start to vary these things over time? That is a tough one, but one we got to tackle.

Ms. BLUNT ROCHESTER. Thank you. My time is expired.

Mr. RATCLIFFE. I thank the gentlelady. The Chair now recognizes the gentlelady from Texas, Ms. Jackson Lee, for 5 minutes.

Ms. JACKSON LEE. I would like to thank the Chairman and the Ranking Member and the collaborators on the House Committee on Education for a very important collaboration, if you will, on a very important issue.

I want to take a moment of personal privilege to acknowledge Dr. Stephen Cambone for his representing a Texas institution, Texas A&M, and as well to thank him for hosting the Hurricane Harvey event in collaboration with the George H.W. Bush Library and to historically host five of our living presidents. So it was a monumental and much-needed event for all of the people that are suffering, and it is well-known in my community that we are still in dire straits and are in certainly need of restoration and resources to do so.

I was speaking to some people in the power industry, and they were trying to explain the Achilles' heels in Puerto Rico in particular, and certainly I think the same kind of Achilles' heel would be present in the U.S. Virgin Islands. One of the issues, of course, is the lack of power and the long journey of having that power back on.

I connect it to the extent of what we are trying to do here is—
our committee, that is in collaboration is the cybersecurity and infrastructure. We certainly need the talent that can relate to those
aspects of our Governmental responsibilities and private-sector responsibilities, and we need the personnel to be able to do so. So I
may have just two questions, and I will frame it in that way.

Puerto Rico needs not only people who know how to work with
hardware, engineers, and those who work with the Army Corps of
Engineers, but we need ideas, we need to understand how we can
protect the infrastructure or the cyber infrastructure that also is a
victim of Hurricane Maria and Hurricane Irma, as well.

So as you answer the question, I think I would like to hear you
talk about the pervasiveness, the wide breadth and depth of cyber,
and the need for human resources in that area to be creative in so
many of the obstacles that we may face, whether it is man-made
or, God forbid, man-made, we hope not, but natural disasters that
we are facing and seemingly are going to face for a long period of
time. We have not yet been able to assess what the fires in California in terms of infrastructure, cyber will do.

The second part of my question is—and I serve as the Ranking
Member on the crime terrorism and Homeland Security Committee, and when we are really at our best in Judiciary, we are
working on ways to prevent crime, to intervene in that, and to find
alternatives for those individuals whose lives are somewhat ruined
for a good period of their life, if they are not rehabilitated. We find
in these incarcerated State and Federal prisons very bright people.

So I would like you to comment on that broad expanse of how
this idea of the work force and building the work force and finding
people to be in the work force, whether it is DACA young people
or otherwise, is crucial to the future of this Nation. I commend for
your reading H.R. 935, which is a bill that I introduced that I am
trying to hopefully draw the attention of the Ranking and the
Chairperson of all of the committees involved here, cybersecurity
education and the Workforce Enhancement Act to prepare in particular minority students and professionals for the jobs of this century.

It goes on to talk about recruiting, providing grants for training
programs, supporting guest lecturer programs. We are using Department of Homeland Security cyber personnel to go out and really get their hands around this issue. So if you would, all of the witnesses, Dr. Cambone—is it "Camboney" or "Cambone"?

Mr. CAMBONE. "Cambone."

Ms. JACKSON LEE. Pardon me?

Mr. CAMBONE. "Cambone."

Ms. JACKSON LEE. Cambone. Dr. Rapp, Mr. Rapp, Mr. Jarvis,
and Mr. Ralls, if you could comment on those points, broad points.

Mr. CAMBONE. Well, thank you, ma'am. I will convey to the chancellor your compliments. As you know, he been assigned the responsibility by the Governor to lead the recovery efforts in the
State. He has done that in coordination with industry, with the
other universities, and brought to bear, because I see them every
day, the two institutions I have made mention of, both TEES and
TEEX. So there is a ready-made force there that we were able to

bring to bear. We need to be able to replicate that around the country.

Ms. JACKSON LEE. Just each one go down and answer the question.

Mr. RAPP. I believe that, you know, as we address cybersecurity and infrastructure that we need to take a look at private partnerships, public-private partnerships like the Battery Innovation Center, working on stored energy and microgrids, so that when we see a natural disaster that takes place or we have a natural disaster, something that takes place, then the grid is not only protected, but segmented and able to come up quicker.

So my point to that is, there is existing technology and partnerships that are working on those types of things out there right now that certainly can be leveraged.

To your other point, I absolutely agree and some of the discussions that we have had in the cyber leadership allowances, how do we reach people who have—are part of the criminal—have been indoctrinated in the criminal justice system that have valuable skills that they can be re-educated and apply themselves to? I think a lot of that can come from great programs into—that are interjected to our places where people are incarcerated.

Ms. JACKSON LEE. Thank you.

Mr. JARVIS. Yes, I don't have anything else to add.

Mr. RALLS. I would add, we have been batting around numbers, statistics related to the already huge gap that we have in terms of demand, supply, in terms of workers, but that has primarily been traditional cybersecurity. When you are talking about infrastructure, I think it brings to mind—or something I indicated a little earlier, but I think we are going to see a great acceleration of one of the largest skill gaps, talent gaps, work force gaps we have right now is in terms of the role of maintenance technicians.

Already, industries and facilities, buildings are already struggling in those regards, but I think what's happening with connection and networking devices and facilities and—where your refrigerator is connected, your HVAC system, your PLCs, technicians' roles I think are going to be even more important. So that is why I think also programs like mission-critical operations certifications that were started within community colleges in North Carolina, opportunities to really look at these areas of critical infrastructure, which will provide a lot of job opportunities for folks who wouldn't traditionally see themselves in the traditional IT cyber role, and to meet those needs, I think we are going to have to have the educational resources, but also the breadth to be able to open up the resources to as many talented people as we can possibly find. I think the demands are going to be huge and accelerating because of that.

Ms. JACKSON LEE. Thank you very much. Thank you, Mr. Chairman. Thank you, Ranking Member. I yield back.

Mr. RATCLIFFE. Thank the gentlelady. The Chair now recognizes the gentleman from Virginia, Mr. Garrett, for 5 minutes.

Mr. GARRETT. Thank you, Mr. Chairman. Thanks to the members of the panel. Thanks to my colleague from Texas for going a little bit over, because that let me get my thoughts together. I appreciate it.

It is great to have you all in front of us. Actually, I was out of the room speaking ironically enough with the commander of TRADOC, Training and Doctrine for the military, and specifically about cyber and the threat they are in. So while I am honored to serve on both the Education and Workforce Committee and the Homeland Security Committee, I am going to come at it from a homeland perspective here in my time.

The paradigm that we face as a Nation has changed in a manner more dramatic than any that I can think of in history as it relates to the threat that we face as a Nation. The reason I say that is, throughout history, whether we are mounted cavalry or dreadnaughts or fighter aircraft or nuclear submarines, we could quantify a threat based on a number of platforms, instruments by which an entity might threaten another, and usually then assess the existential nature of the threat or the lack thereof. We can't anymore.

The reason, obviously, is that one individual with the proper training, located remotely, perhaps in their basement, and that might be in Tehran and it might be in Portland, can wreak havoc uncontemplatable perhaps in human history by virtue of the interconnectivity of everything.

We have seen in the Baltic States, as well as in the Ukraine, the impacts of real aggressive cyber attacks. So as we discussed public-private partnerships to prepare our young people for opportunities moving forward, I think it is important to also understand the Government role in this endeavor because of the fact that the threat of the 21st Century really will manifest itself, I think, at a keyboard and not in the cockpit of an aircraft or the driver's cupola of a main battle tank.

So it is particularly, No. 1, Dr. Ralls, I think we might have bumped into one another when I was back in the Virginia General Assembly, so great to see you here. Thanks for the good work you do at Northern Virginia Community College. A little bit biased. Even if you are from Texas A&M, you are awesome, but we have wonderful community colleges in Virginia, where we try to tailor the training that you all give to the employers in the area and the futures of the young people.

But IBM, DEFCON, what DEFCON does is really the private version of what I think we need to do better as a Nation, and that is sort of a constant, perpetual threat and updating of black-and-white lists, et cetera. But the problem is this. When your pay scale is a Government pay scale and the marketplace drives talent based on the ability to receive a financial reward, then we can be assured that the great cyber minds might be working at Deutsche Bank or Honda International, that they might be working at IBM or at DEFCON, but it is hard to envision them in the wonderful Army green that I wore for 6 years, by virtue of the fact that $55,000 a year doesn't drive the best talent.

So how do we engage young people, (A), to enter this growth industry, and then, (B), how do we—understanding market forces—specifically the payment that you receive for being amongst the elite in your skill set, capitalize on the investment in training these young people to protect this country? That is a riddle that I haven't solved yet.

One thing that we have done is try to collocate cyber units in the military near, you know, technology hubs, you know, Seattle, we might have a cyber unit. Northern Virginia, we have National Guard units that are cyber, so that we might have somebody who works for a wonderful corporation that does IT and then gets a pittance 1 weekend a month to come do that. But I would invite specifically Mr. Rapp and Mr. Jarvis to speak to how we integrate the educational opportunities to the National defense needs that I think we have been slow to identify and certainly don't want to identify too late.

Mr. RAPP. I didn't know if it was appropriate to raise my hand and say "pick me, pick me," but I——

Mr. GARRETT. That is—I already picked you.

Mr. RAPP. That is awesome.

Mr. GARRETT. I was in another room watching you. "This guy."

Mr. RAPP. So I live that story. You know, some of the recommendations we made early on to get cyber integrated into the military, first of all, the United States Army—or, I am sorry, the military needs to look at direct commissions, so for skilled professionals. We do the same with doctors. We do it with lawyers. Why wouldn't we do it with cyber professionals?

The second thing is, is we have increased physical fitness standards for special operations groups. Well, why would we expect cybersecurity professionals to have—why do we not have a physical fitness tests that takes into account the MOSs or the job skills that each one of those soldiers have? We have long since judged people across the board on a single standard. That is just not the reality that we live in today.

There is no shortage of patriotic cybersecurity people out there. But age limitations, the commitments of joining the military, those things all become barriers to entry for cybersecurity professionals. The National Guard is a great way to leverage patriotic Americans that do things on the day and then can bring those skills on the weekends. So I would say those are some ways that we can do it.

I don't think there is a shortage of attracting people to those jobs. I think it is a barrier to entry. I——

Mr. GARRETT. So I am over, but I would beg the Chairman's indulgence. So essentially an MOS waiver program to recruit the best and brightest in specialized fields?

Mr. RAPP. I absolutely think that we should. I will give you another personal story. My son was disqualified from military intelligence service because he was colorblind. So now he is studying cybersecurity and psychology on the civilian side, and he will be hired back by the U.S. Government as a contractor, I am sure.

Mr. GARRETT. Thank you, Mr. Chairman.

Mr. RATCLIFFE. I thank the gentleman.

Mr. GARRETT. I apologize to Mr. Jarvis, but I would welcome, if you want to reach out to our office, I would welcome to hear your thoughts.

Mr. RATCLIFFE. Thank the gentleman. Chair now recognizes the gentleman from Illinois, Mr. Krishnamoorthi, for 5 minutes for questions.

Mr. KRISHNAMOORTHI. Thank you, Chairman Guthrie, Chairman Ratcliffe, Ranking Member Davis, and Ranking Member Richmond, for calling this very important joint subcommittee hearing. Thank you to all the witnesses for coming in today. I really enjoyed your testimony.

I think it is fair to say nowhere is the skills gap or the work force skills gap more evident than in cybersecurity. A recent report by Forbes and the University of Pennsylvania estimates that there are 1.4 million unfilled jobs in this field alone. That is why work force development organizations, community colleges, and CTE program administrators need to work together to strengthen our cybersecurity work force pipeline. Americans' safety and economic prosperity depend on it.

I have a few questions. Dr. Ralls, I was very interested to learn that you have successfully expanded your cybersecurity associate's degree program from 50 to 1,500 people in just 4 years. Could you explain the effect this has had on your school's financial standing?

Mr. RALLS. Well, it explains where we are putting many resources. What we have to do in an age of zero sum is, as resources become available, particularly instructional resources but also facilities, so, you know, we have just purchased a new facility in Manassas. We are renovating a facility in Alexandria. We have a new tech center in Reston. So certainly it is a prioritization of resources, because that is where the work force needs are and because we are not growing overall, even though our cyber program is growing. That means shifting resources. So that is a challenge.

Obviously for us, tapping into the rich pool of adjuncts is important. I have to applaud the NSA for helping us with that. Last year, we had 18 faculty members who were able to receive education in certified ethical hacking to gain the certification. They already had the skills, but they need the certification so they can teach people how to get the certification as part of the program.

So those programs that support those efforts are key. Just yesterday, representatives of colleges around the country were meeting with NSA and brainstorming ideas. One of the ideas was about a virtual job fair, really tapping into recent PhDs and others coming out of programs and trying to draw them into programs like ours.

So I think there are programs out there, certainly NSF Cyber Watch, NSA–CAE programs that are helping colleges like ours, and particularly even not so much colleges like ours, but others that are just getting into the cybersecurity game that are important, but as I mentioned before, those efforts have to scale just as we are having to scale to go from the number of students we are providing.

Mr. KRISHNAMOORTHI. Do you find the funding that you receive at NOVA at the Federal, State, and local level sufficient to meet the demand in the classroom?

Mr. RALLS. Oh, absolutely not. I mean, that is——

Mr. KRISHNAMOORTHI. How much does it need to go up?

Mr. RALLS. Well, I can't tell you. I mean, obviously the—well, I should be able to tell you. But, for instance, just think in terms of our cyber program. So we have 1,500 program-placed students, but we are an open-door admissions. So we don't really say to students, "You can't come into our program." It is just that they will run into challenges as we run into challenges in providing their needs.

So that is an ultimate challenge for us. But I will just give you an example. This year, I mentioned, you know, our Perkins funding. We are the 14th-largest college or university in the country. We have a $270 million annual budget, and our Perkins funding that we get for our college this year is $417,000. You know, that is why we are putting all of it, you know, down on—just recruiting women students, female students through IT, because it is—I truly believe this, that I think technical education is one of the biggest gaps between rhetoric and investment across multiple areas is technical education. We have to get more serious about it.

Mr. KRISHNAMOORTHI. Well, thank you for bringing that up. I am the Democratic lead, along with Republican Glenn Thompson, on the renewal of the Perkins career technical education program that unanimously passed through the House. We are hoping that it passes the Senate. It does provide for more funding. We would ask you to urge your Senators to take this up.

The CyberCorps Scholarship for Service Program at the Federal level today only provides stipends to students at 4-year colleges and universities. How can Congress expand current programs to ensure that community college students have access to these critical funds? Dr. Ralls, do you want to comment on that?

Mr. RALLS. Well, there is the—I think it was introduced in the Senate, a bipartisan legislation, the 2017 Cyber Scholarship Act, which actually would expand those efforts to include community college students. So that is a very specific thing that is out there right now.

We have been able to get some students in the programs through our partnerships with like Marymount University and others who have reached with us, so there are some doors that you can go through, through articulation. But it needs to be expanded to include certainly community college students, and that particular legislation does that or proposal does that.

Mr. KRISHNAMOORTHI. Last question. I know I am out of time. But I did want to ask this. Are there any other countries that do a good job of training their cybersecurity work force or, you know, adequately providing for a cybersecurity work force in their countries? We can take answers from any of you.

Mr. RAPP. I would say a leader in that area would be Israel, and that is through a close cooperation between the educational universities, the educational institutions, private industry, and the military. So they have less barriers between those three sectors, and they have very successfully been able to produce the work force to bat about 35 times above their weight, second only to the United States in cybersecurity product exports.

Mr. KRISHNAMOORTHI. Any others?

Mr. JARVIS. I wouldn't say that maybe some examples of people that are doing a good job, but I think we can look to other countries for examples of how they are trying to address their own cyber skills gap, because they do have them. Whether it is in the United Kingdom, where they are setting up a National college for cybersecurity in Bletchley Park, or if it is looking at Singapore, where they are trying to take a look at various vocational models to help bolster their cybersecurity work force. I think we can look to some examples in other countries to help augment what we are trying to do here.

Mr. KRISHNAMOORTHI. Thank you. Thank you.

Mr. RATCLIFFE. Thank the gentleman. I thank all of the witnesses for your insightful and valuable testimony and answers today. I thank the Members for some very thoughtful questions. It is possible that some Members may have additional questions for our witnesses, and if so, we will ask you to respond to those in writing. Pursuant to committee rule VII(D), the hearing record will remain open for a period of 10 days. Without objection, the subcommittees stand adjourned.

[Whereupon, at 4:21 p.m., the subcommittees were adjourned.]

APPENDIX

Question 1a. Given the mission of Texas A&M University System's land grant mandate including its combination of academic instruction, education in emerging technologies, and the engineering extension, how is A&M working to address needs in the public and private sectors?

What strategies is A&M utilizing to implement those approaches?

Answer. The mission of The Texas A&M University System is to provide education, conduct research, commercialize technology, offer training, and deliver services for the people of Texas and beyond through its universities and State agencies. Since its establishment as a land-grant through the Morrill Act, Texas A&M has fulfilled the legislation's time-honored tradition by conducting high-impact research at all levels and bringing forth practical research applications to citizens in Texas and the Nation.

The original principles set forth in the Morrill Act were to teach agriculture, military tactics, and the mechanical arts as well as classical studies so that members of the working classes could obtain a practical education. As technology has advanced and infused into almost every part of our lives, this mission has evolved to include fields such as engineering, public safety, infrastructure and technology. Cybersecurity is a common thread through these areas and demands to be addressed in the public and private sectors in order to support growth and protect systems.

Increasing the resilience of cyber systems found in both the public and private sectors will require a more skillful work force, ground-breaking new capabilities, and innovative policies. Fortuitously, and consistent with its land grant mandate, the Texas A&M University System has undertaken a series of broad-ranging cybersecurity initiatives that, in combination, address all three areas.

Workforce Development

On the educational front of work force development, A&M System faculty and staff are actively engaged in the development of high-impact education and training opportunities for our students. The overarching goal of these efforts is to ensure that the graduates of our programs are properly equipped to address the many ever-evolving cybersecurity challenges they face in their professional lives.

In recent years A&M faculty and staff have developed a wide array of cybersecurity courses and broader cybersecurity curriculum offerings. For instance, over the past 3 years the number of graduate and undergraduate cybersecurity courses offered at the System's flagship institution in College Station has more than doubled from 17 to 35. Additionally, the University's new Cybersecurity minor field of study, first introduced in February 2016, has already attracted nearly 350 students from across the University. It has already become the highest enrollment minor in College of Engineering. This spring, A&M will enroll its initial cohort of students in a first-of-its-kind Master's Degree program that will further the education of undergraduate engineering students with an advanced degree in cybersecurity expertise that they will use to design and build a more secure next generation of smart, interconnected systems.

Early this year, personnel affiliated with the Texas A&M Cybersecurity Center provided cybersecurity instruction to A&M IT and security staff. This instruction was conducted on the prototype for the Texas A&M-based Texas Cyber Range. This range, now near completion, will serve as a vitalized laboratory to support hands-on educational and training experiences for students and employees across the A&M System, and beyond.

Acknowledging that only a portion of a student's learning takes place in traditional classroom settings, A&M faculty have developed a large number of extra-curricular and co-curricular activities that complement, reinforce, and build upon the knowledge and skills our students acquire in the lecture hall. No less than four student-led organizations, focusing on cybersecurity topics, have been formed at A&M in the past 2 years. Students in these organizations have not only learned a great deal but many participate in teams that have competed, with great success, in dozens of regional, National, and international cyber competitions. Finally, A&M faculty and staff have also worked closely with both public and private-sector organizations to ensure that our students have the opportunity to gain valuable experience through their participation in high-impact cybersecurity internships and co-ops. Our students have consistently identified these real-world opportunities as some of their most valuable learning experiences.

To encourage students to pursue cybersecurity studies, Texas A&M University faculty has acquired grant funding for a variety of cybersecurity scholarship opportunities for our students. To date, nearly 25 students have received full or partial scholarships under these programs. The Texas A&M Cybersecurity Center currently has a proposal under review for an NSF Service-for-Scholarships grant. If approved, it will provide full scholarships for up to 40 students beginning fall 2018.

Over the course of the next year calendar year, building on the above described highly successful educational initiatives, the faculty and staff at the College Station campus will increase their engagement with their counterparts the other 10 universities within the A&M system. The goal of these engagements will be to share course materials, curriculum initiatives, and other educational best practices.

Texas A&M also employs two threads that cross-cut the professional and continuing education of (PCE) of cybersecurity work force development. The first includes certifications (which can also be referred to as badges, credentials, or programs) that are typically multiple courses or modules that can be completed either for continuing education or academic credit. Once the designated course/modules are satisfactorily completed (some may require third-party examinations) a certificate will be awarded. These programs may be accredited by States and/or industry associations. Regardless of any external accreditation, industry must have input into the content and delivery platforms in order for the work force development activities to contribute to effective implementation in the public and private sectors.

The second thread is to ensure that all workers, from novice to the cybersecurity professional, possess the required level of knowledge and competency for their specific roles. PCE can also provide preparation for certification testing that entails the study of a prescribed body of knowledge or technical curriculum and may require to be supplemented by on-the-job experience. PCE is applicable to those with and without a degree from an institute of higher education.

It should be noted that PCE work force development in cybersecurity calls for content and delivery methodologies to be developed and delivered based on adult learning models. These tactics require a different, but complementary approach when compared to traditional undergraduate and graduate teaching methods.

Capabilities

On the capabilities front, A&M researchers have long engaged in a wide array of high-impact cybersecurity research projects. With a primary focus on applied research, A&M scholars have developed capabilities that address some of the many cyber threats that target both traditional IT systems, as well as those that target Cyber Physical Systems (including Industrial Control Systems and other internet of things components). A&M scholars have developed a large suite of tools for malware and Advanced Persistent Threat (APT) analysis, which have been used in hundreds of organizations around the world. A&M researchers have also developed innovative malicious cyber infrastructure (botnet) detection and analysis tools, as well as tools that perform Malicious Social Media analysis. These tools have also been used in scores of organizations, in both the public and private sectors.

Notably, the level of cybersecurity research at A&M has increased dramatically over the past 2 years. There has been a three-fold increase in the average number of grants awarded to A&M faculty and an eight-fold increase in the average amount of research funds awarded to these scholars. This year alone A&M University expects to receive awards of no less than $11.5 million for up 8–10 research projects.

Innovative Policies

On the policy front, a proposal, currently under review, would create a System-level agency, the Institute for National Security & Cyber Security Education & Research (INCSER). This institute will be comprised of the Texas A&M Cybersecurity Center, the Texas A&M Nuclear Security Science and Policy Institute, and a yet-to-be-named Cyber Policy Center, associated with the Bush School of Government and Public Service. In addition to facilitating ground-breaking research and innovative security education, training, and work force development, the INCSER will engage in research that will lead to the formulation of high-impact, forward-looking security policies for organizations in both the public and private sector, across the spectrum from local to international. This year the Bush School of Government and Public Service will introduce a graduate certificate in cybersecurity policy, as a complement to their existing certificate offerings in Advanced International Affairs and in Homeland Security.

Question 1b. What metrics has A&M identified or does A&M use to evaluate the effectiveness of these approaches?

Answer. The Texas A&M Engineering Experiment Station (TEES) and the Texas A&M Engineering Extension Service (TEEX), agencies within the Texas A&M University System, have robust student management systems that provide for registration, program completion tracking, distribution, and an educational records repository. This allows individuals and organizations to manage their work force development efforts as well as track overall performance metrics. It is also critical that work force development efforts are evaluated on several levels. Typically, near-term assessments of courses, modules, and/or programs/certifications are completed immediately following the activity. These assessments are useful, but additional content and application evaluations will inform the overall cybersecurity work force continuum. There are several methods of accomplishing this type of detailed analysis. Surveying individual participants to assess far-term effectiveness can offer specific data about how that person applied the content. Additionally, the TEES EDGE (engineering's professional and continuing education management group) can perform more detailed quantitative and qualitative analyses for individual activities and programs as well as private and public organization impact. This type of analysis would contribute to the life-cycle of work force development including informing original market research along with development and deployment.

The Texas A&M University System is uniquely positioned to provide work force development across the cybersecurity continuum with its university components and agencies. These system members have developed and delivered work force development through the following:
- Undergraduate and graduate programs
- Military and veterans
- University and student organizations
- Customized contracts with organizations and industry associations
- Federal and State-funded grants
- Open-enrollment delivery
- Local, State, National, and international deliveries.

Additionally, systems components have worked with public and private-sector organizations to provide research and technical assistance including risk assessments. This experience informs the work force development continuum by contributing current knowledge in real-time.

QUESTIONS FROM CHAIRMAN JOHN RATCLIFFE FOR DOUGLAS RAPP

Question 1a. When the Cyber Leadership Alliance (CLA) approaches a community college to strengthen or create a cyber studies program, what parameters or identifiers help the Alliance pick the schools to approach?

Answer. The Cyber Leadership Alliance has partnerships with numerous colleges. When CLA evaluates a college for partnership, there are several criteria that we evaluate.

DOES THE COLLEGE UNDERSTAND THE CYBERSECURITY ECOSYSTEM AND WHERE THEY FIT?

Demand analysis.—It is important for education institutions to understand the demand for cybersecurity work force. This is their market research prior to developing a cybersecurity program. It is important to understand if the college is using industry studies such as the PWC Global State of Information Security Survey, using data from the National Institute of Standards in Technology (NIST), using tools such as CyberSeek, and other valid academic and industry data.

Core competencies alignment.—Understanding their own core competencies will better determine the type and level of programming they should pursue. If a college is best known for culinary arts, then shifting to a highly technical advanced cybersecurity degree program may not be a good fit. Additionally, a 2-year community college may want to analyze whether a 2-year cybersecurity degree that teaches the philosophical concepts of cybersecurity is a better fit than teaching a 2-year applied degree, certificate, or industry certifications.

Goals and standards.—Colleges considering cybersecurity programming should have clearly-defined goals and standards. When considering partnerships, CLA places great weight on those institutions that seek to become NSA/DHS-designated

Centers of Academic Excellence and those institutions who have or intend to map their curriculum to the National Initiative for Cybersecurity Education (NICE) Cybersecurity Workforce Framework.

Question 1b. What are some of the issues holding a school back offering these courses already?

Answer. Community colleges wishing to offer cybersecurity programming suffer from several barriers to entry.

Talent shortage.—Colleges suffer from the very malady that they are seeking to treat; a lack of cybersecurity talent. With the significant cybersecurity work force shortage and the premium paid for talent, community colleges are in stiff competition for qualified instructors. Community colleges can achieve success in this area by leveraging working professionals in the cybersecurity field as adjunct faculty.

Knowledge shortage.—There is a common misconception that cybersecurity is an extension or subset of computer science or information technology. Colleges can use 7 functional areas and 32 specific specialty areas identified in NIST Special Publication 800–181 to determine programming that best fit their market and competencies.

Difficulty measuring aptitude.—Since cybersecurity has only been recently recognized as an independent vocational area, the traditional methodologies of measuring aptitude are only now incorporating the KSA associated with the field. As an example, a student that exhibits aptitude for coding may not have the aptitude for risk analysis or intelligence gathering—both specialty areas in cybersecurity. This is complicated by the demographics of community colleges that are comprised a much higher percentage of non-traditional students such as adult learners and displaced workers seeking quick pathways to reenter the work force.

Question 2. How can small businesses, or businesses that do not have the resources, for instance to sponsor cyber competitions, participating the cyber work force pipeline?

Answer. There are two areas where CLA encourages entities with limited resources to participate in the development of a cybersecurity work force pipeline.

Sponsoring/Mentoring cybersecurity clubs.—The cost in both time and resources to sponsor and/or mentor cybersecurity clubs and competitions is low. The annual cost of registering a middle or high school CyberPatriot Club is $205 annually and the elementary schools are free. Clubs and competitions also exist at the collegiate level.

Participation in professional cybersecurity-oriented organizations.—Individuals and small businesses with limited resources can become engaged in numerous organizations with a cybersecurity focus. These organizations include the Cyber Leadership Alliance, Infragard (partnership between the FBI and members of the private sector), EC-Council, ISACA, the Information Systems Security Association (ISSA), and the International Association of Privacy Professionals (IAPP).

QUESTION FROM CHAIRMAN JOHN RATCLIFFE FOR DAVID JARVIS

Question. What type of partnerships does IBM have with universities and community colleges?

IBM has a National footprint; how are schools chosen to become partners?

Answer. IBM partners with universities and community colleges in many areas. Our focus on cybersecurity is typically with schools that have established, successful cybersecurity programs or that have a desire to build and/or create cybersecurity programs. IBM is committed to investing in our local communities and has partnered with universities and community colleges in locations where we are growing our company, to collaboratively focus on skills development and better linking education and employment in key technical roles, including cybersecurity.

Listed below are some of our current cybersecurity-related partnerships/programs:

P–TECH Model and cybersecurity degrees

IBM is utilizing the new education model Pathways in Technology Early College High School (P–TECH) in the United States and other countries specifically for cybersecurity and other technology areas. The model has expanded to over 60 U.S. schools and 300 industry partners, with the goal of expanding to 80-plus schools in 2017. P–TECH connects high school, college, and the world of work to prepare students for STEM jobs of the future.

Designed to serve historically disadvantaged populations, the P–TECH 9–14 School Model provides U.S. public school students in grades 9–14 a clear path to post-graduate opportunities that might not otherwise be available. IBM, along with the New York City Department of Education and The City University of New York, created the first P–TECH school in Brooklyn, New York, in 2011. Through P–TECH, students, who are not screened for admission, earn both a high school diploma and an industry-recognized 2-year post-secondary degree at no cost to them or their families. The students are also first in line for jobs with their industry partner.

On the cybersecurity front, IBM is currently working with Excelsior Academy at Newburgh Free Academy in New York (a partnership between the Newburgh Enlarged City School District, IBM and SUNY Orange Community College) and P-TECH@Carver in Baltimore, Maryland (a partnership between Carver Vocational Technical High School, IBM and Baltimore City Community College) on cybersecurity specific pathway programs.

Community College Skills Accelerator (CCSA)

IBM is partnering with community colleges to build the skills of the future through our Community College Skills Accelerator. This program provides access to documented skills roadmaps, access to free IBM tools (including platforms, services, and software), access to IBM mentorship and subject-matter expertise, including collaboration on curriculum review and creation and pathways to employment (including internships and apprenticeships).

Competitions, Symposiums, Career Fairs

IBM supports numerous university-affiliated cybersecurity competitions, conferences, and career-related events by providing IBM cybersecurity experts as keynote speakers, panelists, product demonstrations, and mentors for students in addition to financial sponsorship. Recent sponsorships include:
- CalPoly Pomona Cyber Security & Awareness Fair: *http://www.cpp.edu/cyberfair/*
- HackCU Boulder Hackathon: *https://2017.hackcu.org/*
- National and Regional Collegiate Cyber Defense Competitions (CCDC): *http://www.nationalccdc.org/*
- NYU Cyber Security Awareness Week (CSAW): *https://csaw.engineering.nyu.edu/*
- RIT Collegiate Penetration Testing Competition (CPTC): *http://www.nationalcptc.org/*

Watson for Cybersecurity—University Program

Last year, IBM announced plans to work with leading universities and their students to further train Watson on the language of cybersecurity, including: California State Polytechnic University, Pomona; Pennsylvania State University; Massachusetts Institute of Technology; New York University; the University of Maryland, Baltimore County (UMBC); the University of New Brunswick; the University of Ottawa and the University of Waterloo. Students working on building Watson's corpus of knowledge in cybersecurity will be gaining hands on experience in cognitive security. *http://www-03.ibm.com/press/us/en/pressrelease/49683.wss#release*

QUESTION FROM CHAIRWOMAN VIRGINIA FOXX FOR DAVID JARVIS

Question. The Federal Work Study program helps students finance their postsecondary education, and it is my view that a student's work-study employment should also contribute to his or her career readiness. What barriers currently exist that hinder work-study students from gaining cybersecurity skills through employment at IBM?

Answer. The Federal Work Study program helps students finance their postsecondary education, but barriers hinder work-study students from career readiness such as gaining cybersecurity skills at IBM. Background: The FWS Program provides funds for part-time employment to help needy students to finance the costs of postsecondary education. Students can receive FWS funds at approximately 3,400 participating postsecondary institutions. Hourly wages must not be less than the Federal minimum wage. Average grants are approximately $1,642.

The work that the student performs must be academically relevant to the student's educational program if the position is at a private for-profit employer. The student's work may not displace employees, impair existing service contracts, nor fill jobs that are vacant due to strikes.

Barriers: Due to statutory and regulatory barriers and inflexibility, students are denied the opportunity to use their work-study grants to further their career readiness. The barriers include:
- Low and Career-Hindering Caps on use of grants for paid internships with private-sector employers in a student's area of study (such as cybersecurity internships with IBM and other private-sector employers)
- Restrictions to part-time internships that interfere with full-time placement such as co-operative learning arrangements.

- Arbitrary Federally-imposed diversions of work-study funds for non-career work-based learning purposes that meet the definition of "community service".
- Limitations on funding authorization levels for Federal Work Study and funding allocation based on outdated formulas unrelated to current needs and goals (such as completion rates, costs of attendance, and job location and development programs).

QUESTION FROM CHAIRWOMAN VIRGINIA FOXX FOR SCOTT RALLS

Question. Since 2010, the National Centers of Academic Excellence in Cyber Operations designation has been open to community colleges. However, only 54 community colleges have been recognized by the Department of Homeland Security or the National Security Agency compared to more than 170 baccalaureate institutions. What recommendations would you have for NSA and DHS as they work to improve their outreach and engagement with community colleges?

Answer. Since 2010, the National Centers of Academic Excellence in Cyber Operations designation has been open to community colleges. However, only 54 community colleges have been recognized by the Department of Homeland Security or the National Security Agency compared to more than 170 baccalaureate institutions. What recommendations would you have for NSA and DHS as they work to improve their outreach and engagement with community colleges?

Specifically, because only 54 community colleges have been recognized by DHS as certified programs relative to 170 baccalaureate institutions, you asked for recommendations to improve outreach and engagement by NAS and DHS.

My reply is that I have a general sense that you will begin to see more community colleges become eligible for CAE designation as the program matures and as community college programs mature. The process is very rigorous, as it needs to be, and requires multiple years of program data before colleges are eligible to apply. Because most college cybersecurity programs are relatively young in their program existence, they would just be reaching the threshold for eligibility for the data requirements necessary to attain certification. So in other words, I think that the issue is not as much about outreach, awareness, and engagement, but more the need for programs to "mature" before they can attain the requirements for eligibility. I think it is good to keep the standards high, and as I indicated in my testimony, provide resources as much as possible to DHS and NSA to assist colleges in attaining the certification requirements.

Beside the issue of program maturity of existing community college cybersecurity programs for reaching the program standards, there may be other issues for community colleges in attaining certification standards relative to baccalaureate degree granting institutions: These include:

    1. Articulation.—Articulation (i.c. transfer of cybersecurity credits to senior instutions) may be problematic as many community colleges focus on articulating transfer degrees (AS) to partner institutions as opposed to Applied Associate (AAS) degrees. These transfer degrees are often heavy on general education requirements, light on technical courses—too light to accommodate the comprehensive curriculum requirements in the CAE2Y. Unfortunately, many of these programs at the senior institution level then tend to fall down on the job with respect to instilling the hard skills that may be better obtained at the community college level (more training, industry certification-focused). Senior institutions should be encouraged to build applied cybersecurity degree programs into which AAS degrees can be transferred from the community college, but that can be challenging with respect to accreditation issues.

    2. Community Need.—Community colleges serve local communities. Many State systems and districts will require the college to demonstrate for new degree programs that they have a local work force market before a program is approved. [sic] is difficult, if not impossible, for rural communities where there are not IT or Cyber companies.

    3. Resources.—More resources are needed to provide for faculty professional development. This is especially important for areas that aren't located near large cyber areas as they have difficulty finding full-time and adjunct faculty.

○